CRAFT GIN MAKING

SKY
WAVE
Small Batch
LONDON
DRY GIN
Hand-crafted
and distilled in
Oxfordshire...
42% ABV
500ml ℮
WORLD
20
GIN
AWARDS
WORLD'S BEST
CONTEMPORARY

CRAFT GIN MAKING

Rachel Hicks and Andrew Parsons

THE CROWOOD PRESS

First published in 2021 by
The Crowood Press Ltd
Ramsbury, Marlborough
Wiltshire SN8 2HR

enquiries@crowood.com

www.crowood.com

This Impression 2022

British Library Cataloguing-in-Publication Data
A catalogue record for this book is available from the British Library.

ISBN 978 1 78500 814 6

Typeset by Simon and Sons

Printed and bound in India by Thomson Press

CONTENTS

PREFACE

It's been quite a ride! Just eighteen short months, from attending gin school to our signature gin being crowned the World's Best Contemporary Gin at the 2020 World Gin Awards, and it has been utterly exhilarating. Along the way we have learnt so much about the art and science of craft gin making, and we're delighted to share it with you here.

We have also made many mistakes, from getting the alcohol content horribly wrong to having so much essential oil from the botanicals that our gin turned the colour of milk. We offer all of this to you here, so that you might learn from our experience.

But more important to us than all of this technical knowledge is that we have met some amazing people. Amazing in their skill, amazing in their dedication, amazing in their devotion to their craft, but even more amazing in their willingness to share all of that with anyone who asks. The craft gin industry really is full of people, old and young, who are highly passionate about what they do, and are delighted to share it with anyone who wants to listen. This book is also for them, and to thank them for welcoming us so warmly into the community.

This community is kind, generous and helpful. Take the moment when we were let down by our bottle suppliers who sent bottles but forgot to include corks, four days before the year's biggest gin festival. We had no product to sell. Our neighbouring distillery – and competitor – offered to send us anything we needed. Take also the wonderful 'maverick distiller' who regularly gave of his time and advice (and still does) out of pure love of his craft, to help us solve many of the problems that we hope to help you avoid in this book.

We'd like to think we are now giving some of that back, in the phone calls we regularly take, and the questions in emails that we regularly respond to. This book is part of that. So whether you are an armchair gin lover wanting to know a little more about his or her favourite tipple, or a budding distiller hoping to join the blessed ranks of award-winning master distillers, this book is for you. Take a nip of your favourite juniper-based spirit, sit back, and enjoy.

Rachel Hicks and Andrew Parsons,
Distillers and Co-Founders
Sky Wave Gin
Bucknell, Oxfordshire, April 2020

ABOUT THE AUTHORS

Rachel Hicks is a founder, partner and distiller at Sky Wave Gin, the multi award-winning artisan craft gin company based in Oxfordshire, whose London Dry Gin was crowned 'The World's Best Contemporary Gin' at the highly prestigious 2020 World Gin Awards. Working daily in the distillery she is responsible for the research, creation and launch of two new flavoured gins. She combines her love of distilling and developing new products with her qualification in Food Technology to evolve new spirits. Rachel runs half-marathons for fun, and once drove across the Sahara Desert in a car she bought for £50.

Andrew Parsons is also a founder and partner, and the Master Distiller at Sky Wave Gin. As an engineer by profession, Andrew's expertise is in the science of distilling. He has defined and documented the strict production processes used in the distillery, refining them over time to produce the perfect spirit. At one time or another he has encountered, analysed and solved all the problems described in this book! Andrew takes great pride in the gins they produce, and is always keen and willing to pass on his knowledge to others. He regularly speaks at events for gin enthusiasts on the science and art of gin distilling. He is also a rock drummer, kiteboarder and qualified military mountaineering instructor.

The authors (centre) accepting the award for The World's Best Contemporary Gin, at the World Gin Awards 2020, London.

ACKNOWLEDGEMENTS

We'd like to mention a few names here, of people we'd like to think of as friends, as a 'thank you'. If we've forgotten anyone it is entirely our fault and absolutely no reflection on the level of help or support given, not only as we have written this book but also as we have adventured on our craft distilling journey over the last few years. This list is also in no particular order. To you all, thank you for your welcome and support, and the camaraderie you have shared with us.

Mary and Richard Bateman at Twisting Spirits Distillery
Alex Jungmayr at In The Welsh Wind Distillery
Barney Wilczak at Capreolus Distillery
The team at The Oxford Artisan Distillery
All at the Chalgrove Artisan Distillery
Anne and Jean-Louis at Saint Amans Gin
The team at Papillon Gin, Dartmoor
Debbie Burgess, online gin blogger
Richard Harknett, online gin blogger
All the team at The White Horse, Kings Sutton, Northamptonshire
Melanie and Lucas Boissevain at Penally Abbey Hotel, Pembrokeshire

Finally, a huge thank you to our army of tasters – some professional, a few family, many friends – who have offered their advice along the way.

PICTURE CREDITS

All images are by the authors, except those on the following pages: 9 David Greenwood-Haigh/Pixabay; 10 (top) DCISR; 13 (left) David Mark/Pixabay; 13 (right) Wellcome Images; 14 Wellcome Images; 15 (left) Cocktailtime/Pixabay; 32 (top) The Papillon Dartmoor Distillery; 32 (bottom) In the Welsh Wind Distillery; 33 (left) Innviertlerin/Pixabay; 27 Twisting Spirits Ltd; 40 (bottom) Bronislaw Drózka; 65 (top) Hans Braxmeir/ Pixabay; 65 (bottom left) Scozzy/Pixabay; 69 Rob Luke; 70 (right) Jenny Walker); 71 (top) Debbie Burgess; 72 Holly Killick; 75 (middle) Jenny Walker; 75 (bottom) Anne and Saturnino Miranda/Pixabay; 79 (bottom) Pastel100/Pixabay; 80 Holly Killick; 82 Craig Melville/ Pixabay; 83 (both) Debbie Burgess; 84 ML991/Pixabay; 107 Bridgesward/Pixabay; 109 Cocktailtime/Pixabay; 115 Daniel Beckett; 116 (bottom) Rob Luke; 119 Elephant Gin; 121 (top) Cocktailtime/Pixabay; 121 (bottom) Viktorija Zan.

INTRODUCTION

WHERE IT ALL BEGAN

At the very start of a gin-making adventure there is a surprising discovery: gin begins as a form of vodka.

It becomes gin through distillation or cold compounding with one essential ingredient: juniper. To be called a 'gin', juniper must be the predominant flavour. Alongside this a huge array of botanicals is used to give the many different brands of gin their distinct flavours, recipes that are kept close to the distillers' hearts.

Distilled gin is defined as being a spirit that is produced by redistilling ethanol of agricultural origin, for example grain, potato, or some other 'thing that grows'. This base spirit can have a strength of up to 97 per cent ABV ('alcohol by volume'); at this strength it is harmful to ingest and can cause serious skin and eye irritation. It is distilled in traditional, often copper stills, which can vary from small 2ltr varieties to large 12,000ltr ones, and with a range of natural plant materials where juniper is the predominant ingredient.

To produce a London Dry Gin, which will be the main focus of this book, only water may be added to the distillate after it has come off the still. It must also have a minimum strength of 37.5 per cent ABV. Cold compounding is the alternative method of creating gin, where the botanicals are added to the neutral spirit, so no distilling takes place. This method will be discussed in more detail later. However, distilled London Dry Gin is considered to be the gold standard of gin making, as the skill lies in the distiller getting the recipe right the first time, as nothing can be added afterwards.

Traditional copper alembic pot stills used for the distillation of gin.

The well-known modern-day gin originates from 'Genever', a Dutch spirit made with juniper berries and usually aged in casks. It arrived in this country from Holland in the seventeenth century. It was a huge hit, but with serious consequences that took 200 years to unpick.

So why has there been such an explosion of craft gins recently? This is a tale of David and Goliath – a couple of centuries of history versus some bright young sparks who wanted to make gin. Their story is compelling, and changed the face of gin production in the UK. They took on the law, enforced by HMRC, and won, opening the gates to craft gin making, which has seen such a boom in the UK and across the world. You can read more about it in Chapter 1, but suffice to say, we have them to thank for the incredible range of gins and myriad craft gin distilleries that have sprung up in Britain since their historic victory in 2008.

This book will delve into the world of craft gin distilling, through our own experience of starting and establishing a successful craft gin company, and by way of the stories shared from other craft gin distillers. The distilling world is generally a very close and

Juniper berries are the key botanical in gin.

Experiencing the warmth of gin lovers at Sky Wave Gin's stall at Eweleaze Farm, Dorset.

Highfield Qualifications

***Highfield* Qualifications**

Certifies that

Katharine R Lort Phillips

has successfully passed an assessment in

Highfield Level 2 Award for Personal Licence Holders (RQF)

Qualification number XXX/XXXX/XX

Date of award 11 September 2018

Certificate number XXXXXXXXXXX

South Northamptonshire Council

Course Director *Training Organisation*

Jason Sprenger - Chief Executive
Highfield Qualifications

THE QUEEN'S AWARDS FOR ENTERPRISE: 2016

cea Regulation

Regulated by Ofqual

Corff dyfarnu cydnabyddedig
Recognised awarding body

There are many licences that must be obtained in order to be able to start distilling – the personal licence is just one of them.

supportive community, which helps businesses thrive. The standard process of craft gin distilling, in relation to the London Dry standard, will be discussed, alongside other types of distilling processes such as 'bathtub', the equipment you need, the extensive range of botanicals from which you can choose, the bottles, the labelling, and how it all works together. However, with every successful distillation day there are always lessons to be learned, so you'll be able to read about troubleshooting, when things don't go quite as you expect.

So you may be raring to go now, with great ideas for a unique flavour profile and an arresting name for your gin. But don't forget about licensing, because not only is it illegal to make even the smallest amount of gin on, say, your kitchen table for your own consumption, but there are actually at least six licences to be acquired if you intend to sell your creation. And an exam to sit. And an interview with HMRC. This is all covered later in the book.

So, if you are an armchair gin enthusiast, or a passionate gin entrepreneur with aspirational thoughts of producing your own spirit, then please read on to learn all about the process, with hints and tips along the way and a bit of history for good measure.

CHAPTER 1

A BRIEF HISTORY OF GIN

The history of gin is as colourful as it is long. About 2,000 years ago, as England struggled in the grip of the Roman Empire, it is believed that a Greek physician created a medicine using juniper berries steeped in wine. He swore it fought off chest infections. A thousand years later Italian monks were found to have a medicinal tonic wine infused with juniper berries.

By the sixteenth century the innovative Dutch were producing a spirit called 'genever', the forefather of our modern gin. The big difference is that it was produced by distilling malt wine to 50 per cent ABV. This meant the final product was so unpalatable due to the crude distilling methods available, that junipers and herbs were used to mask its revolting flavour. But it took off, and soon was one of the most popular drinks in the Netherlands.

England, by comparison, was a little late to the party. The gin boom hit England at the end of the 1600s. King William of Orange (of the Netherlands) became King of England, Ireland and Scotland in 1689. In order to bring a little bit of home with him, he introduced Dutch gin, together with new laws allowing for tax breaks on spirit production due to the fortuitous surplus of grain harvests.

King William III of Orange introduced Dutch gin to England in the 1600s.

A busy gin palace bar with customers buying drinks.

Even before the Dutch spirit became widespread across the country, our armed forces, fighting abroad, already had some awareness of its seemingly enviable properties. British sailors witnessed Dutch soldiers with a bottle of the spirit continually to hand, and noted how they seemed braver in battle – and the British sailors wanted a bit of that 'Dutch courage'. Fortunately for them, it was now easily accessible when they returned from their expeditions. Back home, cheaply distilled spirits, flavoured with juniper and herbs to cover the rough flavour, was the new business phenomenon. Dozens upon dozens of gin houses quickly sprang up, as the latest opportunity to make money was seized upon. The drink was an instant hit, and the London gin craze was about to begin.

THE GIN CRAZE

By the mid-1700s gin distillation had reached epidemic levels and was causing serious problems. The poor were drinking the new affordable gin to excess. It helped to mask the misery of their difficult lives, and from a practical point of view, it helped ward off the feelings of cold experienced by the destitute.

A sense of nationalism also boosted the popularity of gin across the country. The people of England turned their backs on French brandy, partly due to the expense, but also partly because of the political and religious conflict existing between France and England at the time.

The huge surge in gin drinking was also driven by the lack of any kind of legal requirements governing who could make and sell gin. The lack of regulation or qualifications needed to create gin fired the boom in production, as anyone with a pot or a bathtub could create a potent product to sell. Unlike today, a would-be distiller didn't need a licence to start his business. Gin distillation became a free-for-all, with all sorts of rogue ingredients being used in the process, including turpentine, sulphuric acid and even sawdust. In London alone more than 10 million gallons of gin were being distilled every year. By 1721, Middlesex magistrates were decrying gin as 'the principal cause of all the vice and debauchery committed among the inferior sort of people'.

The gin boom was blamed for debauched behaviour, especially among the poor: *The drunkard's children* by George Cruikshank.

Mother's Ruin

The easy availability and affordability of gin led to many women drinking it, more so than any other of the more expensive spirits. It contributed to their children being neglected, daughters sold into a life of prostitution, and even babies being given gin to quieten them. The horrific spell under which London's poor had fallen was keenly portrayed in a print by Hogarth called *Gin Lane*. This shows a drunken woman with ulcerated legs taking snuff as her baby falls into the gin vault below. Gin was described as 'the opium of the people' by the historical writer Ellen Castelow in her essay *Mother's Ruin* on the online site historic-uk.com. Many would do whatever it took to get their 'fix' of gin, which kept them warm in the bitter London winters and allayed their hunger pangs. At the time, the huge amount of rough gin being consumed was linked to male impotency and female sterility, which was considered to be the reason for the death rate exceeding the birth rate in the capital at this time.

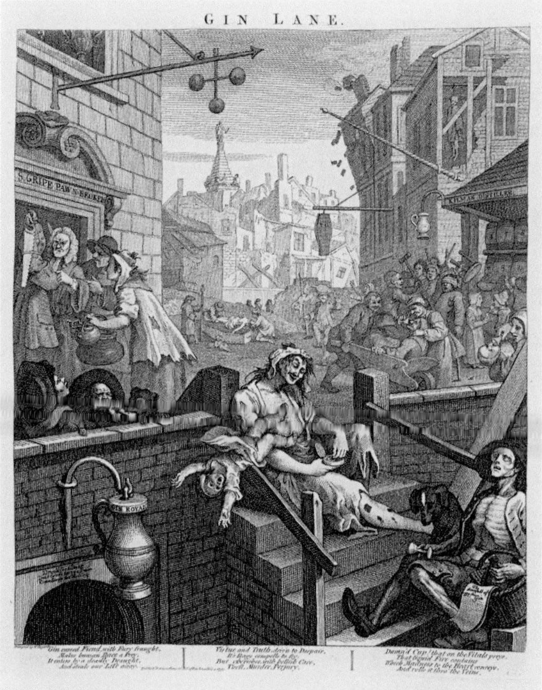

The etching *Gin Lane*, by William Hogarth, is set in the parish of St Giles London, a notorious slum district that the artist depicted in several works around this time. *Gin Lane* depicts the squalor and despair of a community raised on gin.

The 1751 Gin Act

The government had a crisis on its hands. By 1730 it was horrified to discover that the average Londoner drank 14 gallons of spirits each year. Six thousand houses in London were selling gin to anyone who could pay the cheap prices. But this was having a ruinous effect on the population, who suffered ill health and madness through addiction, and drove up crime and prostitution rates.

By 1730 the average Londoner drank 14 gallons of spirits each year.

In 1751 the Gin Act was passed, its intention being to crack down on the consumption of spirits. It required distillers to have a licence, and allowed them only to sell to licensed retailers. As a result, the production of better quality gin increased, and consumption certainly fell. London distilleries strove to produce improved gin, and the capital became known for the quality of its product, hence the term 'London Dry', which is today held as the pinnacle of gin production. At the same time the traditional drink of the nation, beer, was being promoted again, alongside the consumption of tea. By the early part of the nineteenth century the price of beer was lower than that of gin for the first time in over a hundred years, and the gin craze was over. For now...

THE END OF THE GIN ACT

The 1751 Gin Act had huge repercussions, which stretched over 200 years. It changed the profile of gin drinkers from the poorest, who consumed it in huge quantities, desperate for the escapism it offered, to a drink that was sipped by the smarter classes wanting to enjoy the now more expensive and refined tipple. It also changed the way it could be made. The 1751 Gin Act banned production in any still with a capacity of less than 1,800 litres. So the thousands of small, illicit gin-production houses were now breaking the law and they went out of business, making way for large-scale businesses that monopolized production. Gordon's, Greenhall and Plymouth gin were all first distilled in the second half of the eighteenth century. Nothing much changed, then, for over 200 years – until 2008.

Two lifelong friends, Sam Galsworthy and Fairfax Hall, who wanted to revive the outstanding quality of London Dry Gin by opening their own distillery in the capital, discovered they couldn't, as they weren't big enough. But they refused to accept that they had to distil a minimum of 1,800 litres as the law required them to. They were up against the big boys, and they wanted to play by their own rules. So they challenged the law, in the shape of HMRC. They fought it and lobbied it and didn't give up. In 2008, after two long years of legal battles and in a historic victory, the Gin Act was rendered null and void, and the future of gin production in the UK was forever changed. In 2009 Sam and Fairfax opened the first distillery in London for almost two centuries. It was called Sipsmith.

This momentous change in the law has opened up the gin market to a vast array of small and large, artisan gin distillers. Once again the gin arena is changing as the market is flooded with a dizzying array of varied, hand-cut gins. The quality and range of gins produced in the UK is growing exponentially, and this trend is being replicated across the world. As gin lovers continue to explore their favourite spirit and discover myriad choices of quality, handmade gins, distilled with passion and great artistry, it's worth remembering that this wasn't even possible just over a decade ago.

And where will it stop? Gin consumption grew more than any other alcoholic drink in 2018 according to the IWSR, the leading supplier of data and market intelligence on the alcoholic drinks market. In Britain, gin sales grew by 32 per cent in 2018 compared to the previous year. The ISWR put much of this growth down to pink gin. Even Gordon's has bowed to the popularity of the pink tipple and introduced a pink gin. Until then you had to make your own by adding angustora bitters!

The growth of the gin market continues unabated. The richest man in the world has dipped his toe in the water, via his online retailer, Amazon, announcing the launch of its own gin. Sales of gin soared by a staggering 750 per cent in 2019, and there is a dizzying array of choices for the innocent drinker who wanders into a pub in search of a simple gin and tonic – there are seventy-eight brands from which to choose, and it is still one of the most popular drinks on the market.

By the end of 2019, gin was the UK's second largest spirits category, according to Jonny Peacock, customer development, strategy and planning director for Pernod Ricard UK. There are now over 300 gin distilleries in the UK, and while we are not quite consuming 10 litres per person annually as we did in the 1700s, the market is booming. However, this doesn't necessarily bode well, and the situation presents a number of issues.

Too Much of a Good Thing?

With the proliferation of new gins being produced, the quality of the commercial offering has widened immensely. It has been likened to the French wine industry, where some of the best wine in the world is made, and also some of the worst. It could be said that the same is true for gin, that it's easier now to get poor gin, but it's also easier to get very good gin. Undoubtedly some of the care and passion being poured into creating handmade gins delivers some fabulous, complex new drinks. However, with relatively easy access to entry level distilling, a huge amount of less good gin is being created, some may say in order to cash in on the gin bandwagon. As the gin craze continues it can be observed that some drinkers are more inclined to want to consume the next 'new' thing in gin, rather than concern themselves too much with the taste.

This leads on to the dizzying array of gins now available, which push the boundaries of what has traditionally been classed as gin. Flavoured gins and coloured gins are the fastest growing categories. Twenty years ago, a pink gin was flavoured and coloured with bitters – now 'pink gins' are ubiquitous, popping up on every advertising hoarding board and plastered all over Instagram. Even one of the grand-daddies of gin, Gordon's, found itself turning out a pink gin in 2019, alongside a vaguely rosy-looking Hendricks 'Summer Edition'. It was as though these bastions of 'traditional' gin were finally pushed by the shouty youngsters into submission. Whether it is chocolate-flavoured gin or colour-changing gin made with the tears of mythical beasts, the boundaries of what defines gin have been stretched more in the past ten years than the previous three centuries.

Pubs and bars now proffer groaning shelves, overloaded with dozens of different gins in an attempt to keep up with consumer demand for the next new gin. Drinkers in hostelries up and down the land are now faced with gin menus as well as the more traditional wine list. In The Feathers Hotel in Woodstock, Oxfordshire, the gin menu is a book. It has to be, as the Gin Bar in the hotel offers a variety of over 400 gins from around the world. It was the first bar into the *Guinness Book of World Records*™ for offering the greatest selection of gins on the planet.

So where does that leave the humble gin drinker? Many are thrilled at the kaleidoscopic choice of gins, finding that the sweeter, flavoured gins allow them entry into the hugely hip gin-drinking club, once denied them on the basis that they didn't like the taste of, for example, a traditional London Dry Gin. However, for the purists, the explosion of flavoured, coloured and even glittery gins is merely a lot of noise and distraction from the considered art of creating a complex gin, with subtle flavours, using traditional methods and, most importantly, being juniper led.

100
150
40
60
20
THERMOMETER
80
200
0
100
-20
120
Hillbilly Stills
°C
°F
Copper King
250
SAFETY GLASS

CHAPTER 2

INGREDIENTS, TOOLS AND EQUIPMENT FOR MAKING GIN

Making your own craft gin can be as simple or as complex as you wish to make it. Most people start small with just a few bottles at a time, and use the simpler method of gin making called cold compounding; others may wish to dive in with the big boys and girls from day one, and distil. Therefore the ingredients and equipment you need will vary greatly, depending on what you decide to do. This chapter starts with cold compounding and leads up to distilling, so the ingredients and equipment are described accordingly.

COLD COMPOUNDING

Cold compounding has been mentioned in the Introduction, and in fact most people are familiar with the process without necessarily realizing it – we all know people, perhaps even ourselves, who have made, for example, sloe gin by steeping sloes in some cheap supermarket gin in the bottle. Well, that is basically cold compounding. The only difference between making a craft gin as opposed to flavouring someone else's is that you won't start with gin – your process should involve making the gin itself too!

To cold compound home-made craft gin, you will need some ingredients but very little equipment.

Basic Ingredients

A Neutral Base Spirit

The easiest way to get a neutral base spirit when you are starting off is to use plain, unflavoured vodka – the plainer the better. Gin is made from a neutral spirit, often grain spirit, and this is exactly what vodka is. Vodka can be made from a variety of base ingredients in addition to grain, so take your pick from, amongst others, molasses, grapes and potatoes. Purists tend to use grain spirit. Try to ensure that the vodka is at least 40 per cent ABV (alcohol by volume), for reasons that will be discussed later.

It is also possible to obtain small quantities of grain neutral spirit from online suppliers such as Master of Malt – just search for 'grain neutral spirit', 'GNS' or 'NGS'. But be prepared for its price to be a shock, as it will be at a higher ABV than any vodka (possibly as high as 70 per cent). As it is excise duty paid and the tax is based on the alcohol content, the price will reflect this.

The Botanicals

The botanicals are the herbs, spices, plants and plant extracts – basically anything that grows – that gin makers use to flavour their gins and make them distinct from the next. By law, in commercial products, the predominant flavour must be juniper in order to call it gin on the label, otherwise you're just making flavoured vodka; as a rule of thumb, this means that at least 50 per cent (by weight) of the botanical content must be juniper. But beyond this rule – which, if you're not planning to sell your gin, can happily be broken! – you have infinite choices on what botanicals to use. The exact botanicals and their quantities are your gin recipe: your creation, your closely guarded secret. It is this, more than anything else, that will create the character of your gin. The wide topic of botanicals will be discussed in more detail in Chapter 4.

Equipment

A Suitable Container

A large Kilner jar, ideal for cold compounding initial experimental recipes. Ensure that you shake or stir regularly to extract as much of the essential oil as possible from the botanicals.

If you are making just one or two bottles at a time, which is appropriate when you are developing your recipe, a large Kilner jar is perfect. If you want to make larger quantities, then beer-brewing tubs of the kind illustrated are ideal. Tubs of 25ltr and more are available.

Spoons and Stirrers

You will need a variety of implements such as metal spoons or other stirrers – metal is considered better than plastic in spirits production as some believe that plastic, even food grade, can impart unwanted flavours.

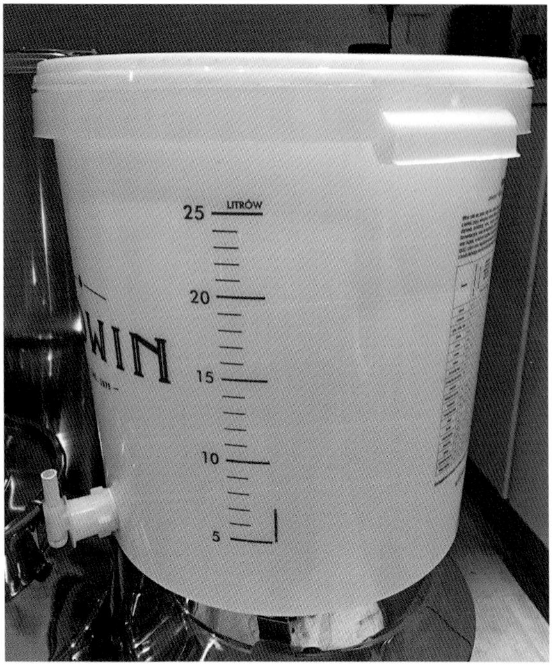

A 25ltr beer brewing tub. Tubs such as this are useful for producing larger quantities of compounded gin, and for macerating fruit for fruit gins. They are usefully marked in 1ltr gradations, which is helpful for ABV and volume calculations.

A Means of Filtration

Because in cold compounding the botanicals are steeped directly in the spirit, we need to filter the product before bottling. Various methods are available including muslin, widely available wine filtration bags, coffee filter papers and washable metal coffee filters, as well as professional filters used with bottling systems.

Bottles, Stoppers and a Funnel

Bottles are available online from very many craft outlets. Choose your bottle wisely, as it will become part of your gin legend, your brand. Stoppers come in synthetic or natural cork versions, the latter being more expensive. Funnels are widely available, but

Bottles come in all shapes and sizes; the shape you choose will become part of your brand. Stoppers may be synthetic or natural – each has advantages and disadvantages. Funnels are used regularly throughout the production processes, and a variety of sizes will prove useful.

make sure you choose an appropriate size for the neck of your bottles, and ensure they are made from food-grade materials.

Extra Equipment

The equipment above really is all you need to get started if you intend to give away your gin or drink it yourself. But if you want to go further, perfect your recipes and understand more about what you have created, you may also want to consider procuring the additional equipment described below.

Glass Beakers

A variety of glass beakers, of the kind you may remember from school science lessons, are useful for collecting, sampling, inspecting and testing your gin, and again are available online. They should have an accurate scale on the side, and if you want to bottle your gin in order

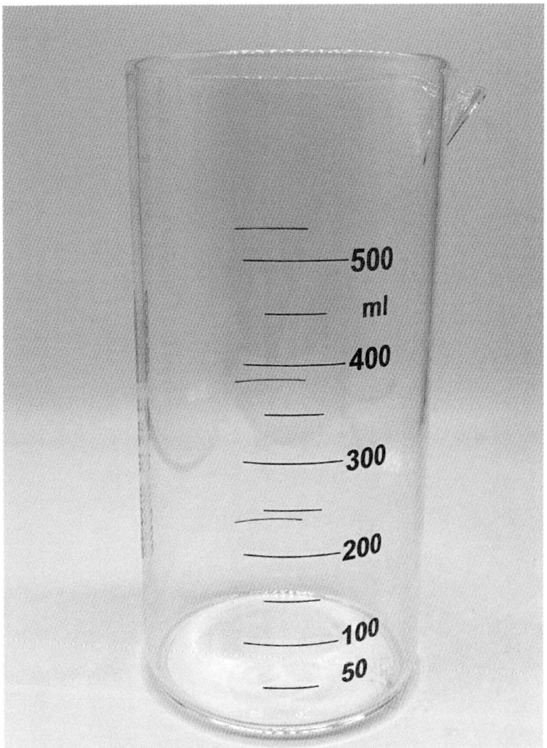

Stamped measuring jars are used for precise, certified volume measurements. Jars such as this are UK government stamped to certify that the ml markings are highly accurate.

to sell it, you may need a volumetric measure that is government stamped to a certified volume.

A Sampling Jar, Alcohol (Spirit) Hydrometer and Thermometer

These items will be needed to determine the alcohol content of the gin you have created. Make sure the hydrometer is an alcohol hydrometer and not a normal hydrometer, to avoid having to do too many calculations. An alcohol hydrometer is already calibrated specifically for alcohol, whereas a normal hydrometer is calibrated for water. The thermometer is necessary because most spirit hydrometers are calibrated to be accurate at 20°C. If the spirit you are measuring is off this by even a few degrees, the results can be very wrong.

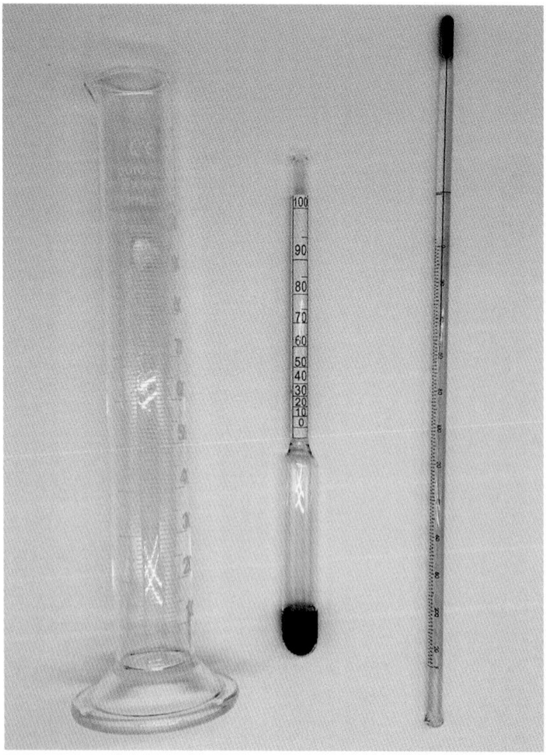

Sampling jars are used when measuring the ABV and temperature of samples of distillate and cut gin. The jar is filled with liquid to be tested, and the alcoholmeter is floated in the jar to give the ABV reading. The thermometer is used to determine whether any temperature corrections are needed.

DISTILLING

When you move on to distilling your gin, the ingredients remain the same (with one addition, and one variation, *see* below), but there is a step change in your basic equipment needs. Instead of merely a container in which to steep your botanicals, you need a still. Stills have been around for thousands of years, possibly invented by the Arab peoples of North Africa (as seen in the alembic style of today).

You will need the equipment described in the following section.

The classic alembic still, one of the oldest still types in the world, is the entry point for most craft distillers. Relatively simple to use, it is a great tool with which to perfect the art. The authors still use this exact still for product development.

The Still and Associated Equipment

The Still Itself

The still you use will probably be a pot still, with a kettle, swan neck, lyne arm and condenser. Many people will choose a copper still, which itself is a work of art. As before, a small number of suppliers can be found online. Portuguese-manufactured stills are highly sought after. For experimenting and initial production, a still size of 2½–5ltr is more than large enough. You may wish to upgrade to a larger still if you intend to produce greater quantities in due course, but it is not really practical for the craft distiller to develop recipes on a large still because of the costs involved in the raw ingredients, particularly the neutral spirit. A smaller still is also easier to operate and control. It is therefore recommended that you use a smaller still initially as you perfect your recipe and your techniques.

The Heat Source

All stills require a heat source of some sort. Traditionalists may prefer a direct flame, but an electric hotplate, as shown here, allows the still temperature to be thermostatically controlled.

For control reasons many people prefer electric heating methods that are usually managed using a thermostat, and many pot stills can be bought with, or used with, hot plate-style heaters. However, purists may prefer to use a more traditional heat source, and some stills can be used with burners.

Collecting Jars

The glassware mentioned earlier would be suitable as collecting jars.

Water Source and Piping

The distillation process requires that the vapours coming off the still are condensed. This is achieved using a condenser as part of your set-up; it needs to have a continuous flow of cold water passing through it, so you will need a source of cold water (a tap), appropriate tubing from the tap to the condenser, and more tubing from the condenser outlet to a drain. Food-grade tubing from the spirit outlet of the condenser to the collecting glass will also be needed.

The Additional Ingredient

The additional ingredient needed when you distil your gin, as opposed to cold compounding, is water. When using the distillation method, the distillate that comes off the still will be far too strong to drink! Depending on the efficiency of your still, it could be anything from 70–85 per cent, and it would be dangerous to consume this. Therefore you need to add water to cut it back to the strength you wish to bottle it at. Again, the law requires this to be at least 37.5 per cent ABV, which you must meet if you wish to go public with your gin. Most craft gins are at least 40 per cent ABV, but it is your choice: the lower the ABV, the further your distillate will go, but the more watered down it will feel on the mouth.

The choice of water is very important as it can alter the character of the gin. Choose a neutral distilled or spring water that isn't too heavy in minerals to ensure that the flavour profile can shine through.

The Varied Ingredient

Instead of using vodka as the base spirit, once you start distilling you might like to use genuine neutral grain spirit (or NGS, as it is known). This is much purer than using vodka and will have absolutely no flavour, thus making the gin 100 per cent yours. It is usually sold in a minimum of 25ltr containers, at 96 per cent ABV, and as such needs careful handling because at these concentrations it is dangerous for skin and eye contact, and highly flammable. HAZMAT and Health and Safety legislation applies, which you must research and familiarize yourself with. You will also need to be registered with the government's Alcohol Wholesalers License Scheme to buy NGS like this in the UK; similar regulations apply around the world. NGS is discussed in more detail in Chapter 4, and licensing in Chapter 9.

Other Equipment

Your extra glassware, and your sampling jar, alcohol (spirit) hydrometer and thermometer become critical when using the distillation method because you need to be able to tell exactly the alcohol content of the spirit that comes off your still.

The glassware marked with volumetric scales now also becomes vital. To calculate how much water to add to your distillate to cut your gin to your desired ABV, you need to know exactly how much distillate you have produced, and be able to measure precisely the quantity of water to add.

FURTHER EQUIPMENT FOR YOUR DISTILLERY

As you increase your competence in the craft, and produce delicious gins that you wish to share with friends, family and everyone else, you will need to improve your storage capabilities and ramp up your ability to bottle. You will also want to label your bottles. You may therefore start to think about the additional equipment described in the following paragraphs.

Storage Vessels

The best – some might say only – storage medium for larger volumes of spirits waiting to be bottled is without doubt food-grade stainless steel. Various churns and containers are available, and again, an online search will reveal a wide variety. It is important that your containers are made from 316- or 430-grade stainless steel to ensure that it is of good enough quality for storing a product for human consumption; if there is a choice, 430 is marginally the better of the two for spirits, and can be slightly cheaper. Most UK, US and

Sooner or later, all craft distillers need a variety of storage vessels: food-grade stainless steel for gin, food-grade PET for flavoured products. This image shows a PET container of fruit gin, and a variety of stainless-steel churns and drums.

European manufacturers will offer very high quality products in either grade, but they can be expensive. Far Eastern manufacturers can offer considerably cheaper alternatives, but it is vital to ensure that the products do meet the grade – literally.

Initially you may need two or three small to medium-sized containers (around 25ltr). When deciding how many you might need, think about what you need them for – for storage, obviously, but also for blending and cutting your gin.

Food-grade plastic containers are a massively cheaper alternative, but some people believe they can impart a flavour to the gin. Use them sparingly, and only for products with a strong flavour of their own. We recommend that subtle gins should not be stored in them.

Bottling

Initially you will probably bottle by hand using a funnel and filter (we recommend that all bottled spirit passes through at least one filter). However, bottling more than about twenty bottles at a time this way will quickly become tedious, and you will want to invest in a bottling machine. Vacuum bottling machines serve three purposes: they take the strain out of bottling by removing the need for pouring through a funnel, and speed up the process dramatically; they allow an in-line filter for much better filtration than something placed in the funnel; and they allow precise setting of volumes in each bottle. Entry-level machines that enable the filling of about 100 bottles an hour, and filter in line, are available. One such machine, made in Italy, can be sourced from a number of companies for around £500.

OTHER CONSIDERATIONS

Licensing

Technically it is illegal to distil gin in the UK without a licence, known as a rectifiers licence, even for your own consumption. It is even illegal to cold compound – including the sloe gin you make at Christmas! A wide variety of licences is needed, depending on what you intend to do, and whether and to whom you intend to sell. Chapter 9 goes into more detail about the licences needed and how to apply for them, but this chapter wouldn't be complete without drawing your attention to them.

Botanicals

The flavour in a gin comes from the botanicals chosen to infuse or distil into it. Remember that, for it to be a gin at all, the predominant botanical should be juniper, but outside this, the world is your oyster regarding the choice of botanicals. But what actually is a gin botanical? We delve more deeply into botanicals – what they are, how they work, and how to develop your gin through your choice of botanicals – in Chapter 4.

A selection of some common gin botanicals. Clockwise from the bottom left: dried rose petals, juniper berries, cloves, coriander seed, dried orange peel, dried lavender. Many distillers prefer to use fresh rather than dried ingredients wherever possible.

Additional Infrastructure Requirements

Assuming you won't be cold compounding your gin and will wish to distil at some point, there are certain infrastructure requirements for even the smallest of distilleries. To operate any kind of still, as described above, running water will be needed for the condenser. A still with an electric element or hot plate will need mains electricity. And if you intend to sell your gin, or indeed give it to anyone except yourself, then stringent hygiene requirements will be required for your workspace.

Experience suggests that you will need a decent amount of space for your distillery. In addition to the footprint of the still and the working area around that, you will also need room for cutting and blending, bottling and labelling, cleaning the still and containers, and the storage of all ingredients, bottles, packaging and products waiting to be bottled. Therefore choose a space that is more than large enough for your current needs, and where there is plenty of room to expand.

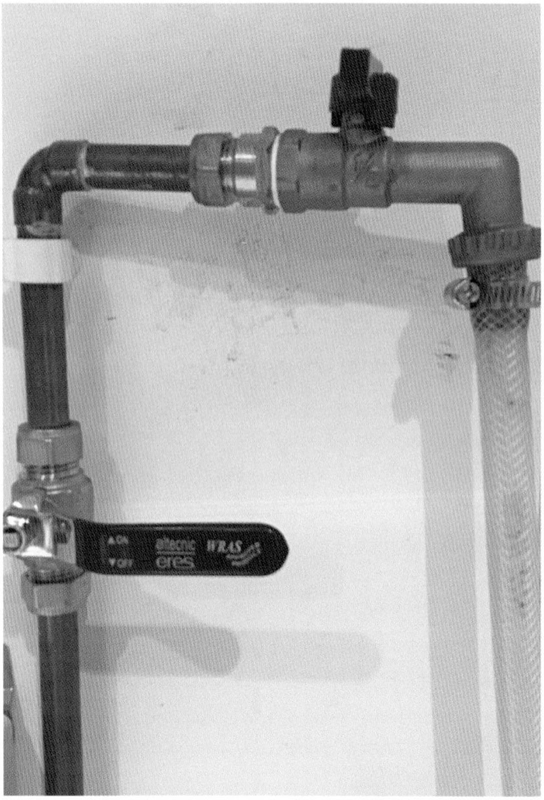

A typical mains cooling water installation for the condenser for a still. Note the multiple taps to allow isolation and easy component replacement if necessary.

Water

A reliable water supply is critical to successful distilling. For a small still, a tap and sink will suffice if the still can be situated in its vicinity. An adaptor will be needed for the tap (similar to a hosepipe adaptor), and a hose of the right diameter for the inflow and outflow pipes on the condenser on the still. You must also be able to dispose of the outflow down a sink or drain. We have even used a set-up for mobile distilling where we ran a long hosepipe from a tap and collected the outflow in containers, and disposed of it by hand! Remember that this water does not come into direct contact with the gin, so the tubing doesn't need to be sanitary or sterile.

For larger installations you will want to consider having pipework installed, terminating close to where the still will be sited. Unless you are a DIY expert, you should use a professional plumber who will be able to advise you on the best options. A mains water source will be needed, and a means of outflow to a drain.

Power

If a still is used with a built-in heating element, or with a hot plate (as opposed to one with a burner), then a power socket will be needed. Small stills will usually use a standard 13A plug and will draw no more current than a kettle. However, larger stills will draw much more current (often 5.5kW or more) and will need a more industrial power supply, able to deliver in excess of 30A. You should consult a qualified electrician for such an installation.

Hygiene Requirements

If you intend to sell your gin, you will need to meet the statutory requirements for products for human consumption; this means that you must meet food hygiene standards. You must therefore have a working area that you are able to keep meticulously clean. Consider an area that is, or can be, tiled, with working surfaces and floors that can be easily and properly cleaned.

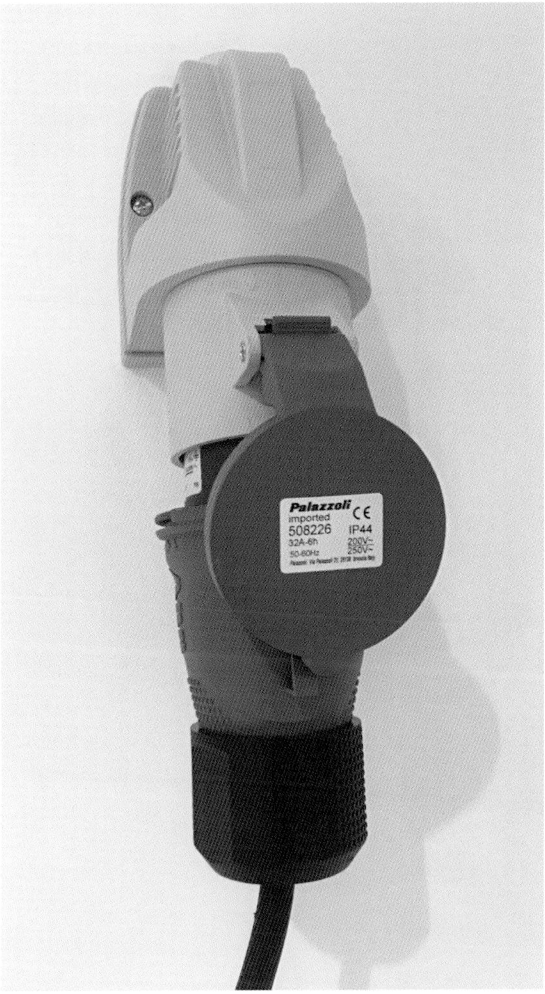

Most production stills (of 30ltr or more capacity) with electric heating elements will draw significantly more current than a standard domestic 13A socket can provide. 32A sockets such as this will be required and must be professionally installed.

BOTTLES AND PACKAGING

The final section in this chapter looks at what is needed for the end product: bottles and packaging. This is a key area for your brand, and one that you will want to get right. At first you might not care about how professional your product looks – you just want your friends and family to try it. If that is the limit of your ambition, then so be it; choose any suitable bottles you may have lying around, or which you can get from craft outlets on the internet. Indeed, a mixture of bottle shapes and sizes may be quirky and just the effect you want. Hand-written labels with the title and date may take you back to childhood days of damson jam, and can be equally fun.

In due course, though, you may want to make your gin appear more professional. You will need to choose a bottle shape, and a supplier you can depend on to supply them regularly and quickly. You will also want to think about your labels – their design, and having them printed. Both are extremely important considerations.

For choice of bottle, do you want to be traditional, with a porter-style gin bottle, or more distinctive – or even quirky? This is entirely your choice, but it is worth thinking ahead to when you might wish to automate (or semi-automate) your filling and labelling processes. Square or unusually shaped bottles are difficult for machinery to handle, and you will be in the realm of specialist devices, which can add significant cost. A simple, round bottle is much easier to use with filling and labelling machines.

You should also think about bottle size, or sizes. Will you offer a large but traditional 700ml bottle, or emphasize your craft credentials with a 500ml bottle? Craft gin will never be as cheap or easy to make as mass-produced gin, so many craft distillers stress how small their batches are by only offering it in smaller bottles such as 500ml and 350ml.

You may also want to offer choice in sizes, such as 500ml, 200ml and 50ml options. It is therefore important to choose a bottle family that offers the same bottle in these different sizes if you want to achieve a consistent look.

Developing your label – which is effectively your brand – can also be quite a challenge. Assuming you have chosen a name for your gin, which can also be extremely difficult if you're not simply using a geographic approach, you will want a label that displays this as effectively as possible, with some other aspect that makes your gin stand out, and a form of words perhaps to describe your creation. It is well worth drafting a few, if you're artistic, and sharing them around friends and family for an opinion. Most traditional labels are white on dark or dark on white,

Gin bottles come in all shapes and sizes. Your bottle will become part of your brand, so choose your style, size and shape wisely. Note also that anything other than a round, regularly shaped bottle will be difficult to label.

and tend to have lots of scrolls and fills. You will probably have a design in mind, but do listen to the opinions of others, as the majority opinion does count. It is easy to be blinded by your passionate view, rather than what will actually stand out on a shelf.

Once you have a design favourite – front and back labels, or a full wraparound (but remember you will be labelling by hand, at first at least) – you may want to employ a designer to produce printer-ready artwork. This is well worth the investment, unless you can find a printer who will do this for you as part of their service.

Don't forget to think about stoppers or corks for your bottles. Most suppliers will offer stoppers as part of the purchase of bottles, but these may be of a lower quality than you might want. Some even state that their stoppers should only be used for the storage of upright bottles, and will leak if bottles are on their side – no good if your bottles are being couriered around, when you can't guarantee how they're handled.

You should also consider whether you want synthetic or natural corks. There is much highly passionate debate about this. Synthetic corks are usually a compressed and bonded substance, and you should check carefully if they are suitable for spirits – some are all right, while others can literally dissolve in gin. Natural corks, on the other hand, shout quality – but there is a view that oils in the cork may taint your gin and turn it slightly yellow in colour. A synthetic cork suitable for spirits will not do this – but it doesn't have the same quality feel. It is much like the cork versus screw-top debate in the wine world. The choice is yours.

IN SUMMARY

So in summary, your needs for gin making depend entirely on the type of gin you want to make, and the scale of the operation you intend to create. This chapter has reviewed the equipment and ingredients that will be needed, depending on that choice. The next chapter looks at the various ways that gin is made.

°F
°C

CHAPTER 3

PRODUCTION METHODS

Gin-making methods have evolved considerably since the early rough spirits produced in Holland and Britain in the seventeenth and eighteenth centuries. Simple, inefficient pot stills, coupled with poor ingredients, produced such foul-tasting alcohol that it had to be flavoured somehow just to be palatable. Old Tom gins were one approach, where the gin itself is made by a second distillation of the base spirit, but a more acceptable flavour (especially sugar) is added afterwards. Similarly, bathtub gins evolved where the base spirit is turned to gin by steeping botanicals, including juniper (hence gin), in it, rather than subjecting it to further rough distillation.

Modern stills have exotic-sounding components such as reflux columns and dephlegmators, which add an extremely high level of refinement of the spirit, producing the wonderful and subtle flavours we now enjoy.

This chapter explores gin-production methods, both ancient and modern, allowing you to choose which methods you might wish to employ to produce your spirit. Even the oldest methods are enjoying a resurgence in the gin-making world, and the resulting flavours can be quite distinct.

DISTILLATION

The Still

Distillation, or more technically *rectification*, is the process that produces most of the world's gin. The process is more correctly called rectification because, as we have discussed, gin is made from a wash already containing a neutral alcoholic spirit. The process is therefore re-distilling, or rectifying, existing alcohol.

Distillation takes place in the still. A pot still consists of a heat source, a kettle, a column, a lyne arm and a

A typical alembic still set-up, which may be used by most distillers starting out in craft gin distilling. The key components are highlighted and are described in the text.

condenser, and possibly a thumper. A typical small alembic still, used by many craft distillers as their first still, is of this type, usually without a thumper.

Papillon Gin at the Dartmoor Distillery uses a much larger version of this type of still as their production still, but it is essentially the same.

The picture of one of the stills at the In The Welsh Wind Distillery in Cardigan, Wales, shows a more sophisticated configuration. Although a fabulous bespoke still, it is still a relatively simple set-up with a kettle, thumper (the component in the middle of the picture) and a condenser. Note the parrot on the right-hand end.

An even more complex arrangement used in some distilleries may include a gin basket, a more intricate column with reflux plates, possibly a dephlegmator, a condenser and a parrot.

The kettle contains the wash (sometimes called the mash): a neutral spirit, at anything from around 40 per cent to around 60 per cent ABV (alcohol by volume). The botanicals are added either directly into the wash, or sometimes they are held in a gin basket. This is a container, often copper, with holes, or made of mesh, suspended in the still or still column above the surface of the liquid or, in more sophisticated stills, in the pipework between the column and the next stage of the still.

The gorgeous all-copper traditional alembic still used by Papillon Gin at the Dartmoor Distillery in Moretonhampstead, Devon, England. The kettle is on the left above the heat source. The distiller is lifting off the hood to allow botanicals to be added. He will replace and seal the hood, before connecting the lyne arm to the condenser, which can be seen in front of him to the right.

This magnificent bespoke still, named Afanc after the Welsh river monster, is at the In The Welsh Wind Distillery in Tan-y-groes, Cardigan, Wales. The electrically heated kettle with copper hood is on the left, the thumper is in the middle, and the condenser and parrot are on the right.

A turnkey commercial still showing a steam-jacketed kettle, copper hood, four-plate reflux column, dephlegmator and condenser.

Once the botanicals are in place the wash is then heated. Distillation works because alcohol boils at approximately 78.3°C (at sea level), whereas water of course boils at 100°C. By keeping the temperature of the wash at around 80–85°C, it is possible to boil the alcohol and collect its vapours, whilst leaving the water behind. The alcohol absorbs the essential oils from the botanicals and transports them in the vapours, and the whole is collected as distillate. Believe it or not, in principle at least, it's as simple as that!

Of course, all the extra components do add to the process. The column allows *reflux* to take place. This is where the rising vapour, containing the delicious essential oils from the botanicals, condenses and flows back down the column until it turns into vapour again. In a column with plates, the plates add to the process by providing more surface area, causing even more reflux at the plates themselves. This process of repeated vaporization and condensation causes more and more flavour to be added, until eventually the vapour rises to the top of the column and over into the condenser. The column also results in a very pure spirit, as all impurities from the wash are collected in the column and flow back down. However, the plates can also *strip* flavour, so getting the balance right – the correct number of plates for your process – is very important.

A dephlegmator (sometimes called a reflux condenser) provides a similar function. This is effectively a column but without the plates. It is typically above the plates (but could be below, or might exist on its own), and simply adds another level

An alembic still with alternative hood style, reflux column with dephlegmator and condenser at Panda Gin in Waterloo, Belgium. The different styles of hood allow for different amounts of reflux.

of reflux. If you look at a still column, with the fabulous vertical line of sight glasses, then the part where the column continues but the sight glasses stop, is the dephlegmator. The column is on the left-hand side. Essentially, the more times the alcohol is vaporized, travels up the column and is re-condensed by a reflux component before it makes its final journey up and over the neck of the still, then the more refined the spirit will be – but beware the loss of flavour and the loss of the heavier oils. Some dephlegmators are also cooled – effectively providing a condenser within the column.

A thumper is an ingeniously simple device that adds purity and, if used in a certain way, alcoholic strength. Vapour passes down into the thumper and condenses. Eventually the level of liquid will rise sufficiently that the vapour is injected into the liquid, causing it to heat up. In due course, this liquid will also boil and start to rise up the second tube (towards the condenser). If the priming liquid in the thumper is water, then the thumper will help to purify the spirit – but it will also (initially) reduce the alcohol content in the vapour. However, if the thumper is primed with neutral spirit, especially at a high ABV, then this can make the distillate even more concentrated.

The condenser, the final functional part of the apparatus, usually consists of a tube within a tube. The spirit (initially as a vapour) travels down the inside tube. Cold water flows through the outside tube, normally in at the bottom and out at the top to ensure uniform flow. This cold water causes the alcohol vapour to condense and return to liquid form. It is this condensed liquid – alcohol containing botanical essential oils – that is collected as distillate.

The final piece of equipment sometimes seen on a still doesn't actually make a difference to the distillate in any way. It is known as a 'parrot' because of its shape, and it is there to allow a hydrometer – or more technically an alcoholmeter (because it is calibrated for ethanol, not water) – to be used to monitor the strength of the distillate continuously, rather than having to take samples. An example of a parrot can be seen in the picture from Sky Wave Gin's Bucknell Distillery.

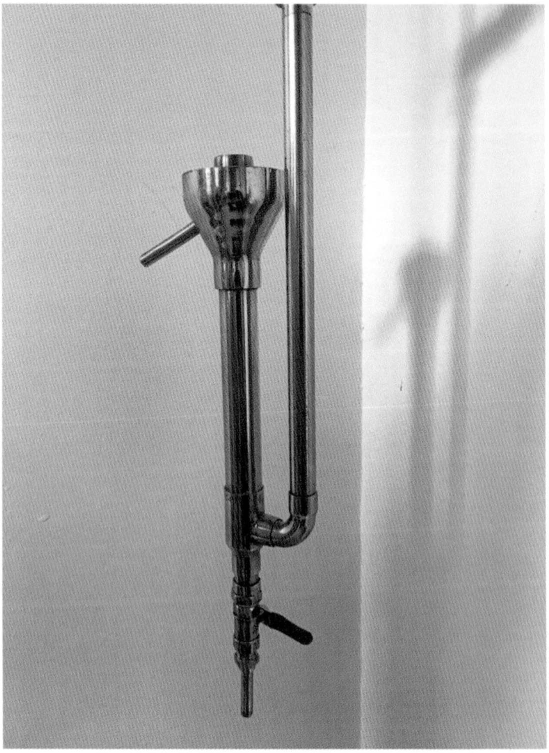

The parrot on the production still at Sky Wave Gin's Bucknell Distillery. The distillate flows into the parrot down the tube on the right-hand side. This fills up the central section, in which the alcoholmeter is floated. The central section (just visible at the top of the top cup) overflows into the top cup, and the distillate flows out from the spout into the collecting vessel. The parrot allows the alcoholmeter to give a constant reading of the ABV of the distillate, rather than having to take samples.

The London Dry Standard and the One-Shot Method

London Dry Gin, or simply London Gin, is defined in EU (and subsequently UK) legislation as follows:

> A type of distilled gin obtained exclusively from alcohol of agricultural origin whose flavour is introduced exclusively through the re-distillation in traditional stills of alcohol in the presence of all the natural plant materials used, the resultant distillate of which contains at least 70 per cent

alcohol by volume, which does not contain added sweetening exceeding 0.1 gram of sugars per litre of the final product, nor colorants, and which does not contain any other added ingredients other than water. The minimum alcoholic strength by volume of London gin shall be 37.5 per cent. Further alcohol of agricultural origin may be added.

(For the technical amongst you, this is paraphrased from Regulation (EC) No. 110/2008 of the European Parliament and of the Council of the European Union of 15 January 2008, Annex II Spirit Drinks, Paragraph 22.)

This means that it must be distilled in a still, all the botanicals must be present in the wash or a gin basket, and nothing can be added afterwards except water (and possibly a tiny amount of sugar).

Sometimes neutral alcohol can be added after distillation, too – *see* the concentrate method described below. However, when no further alcohol is added, this is known as the 'one shot' method, because effectively what comes off the still is what's bottled, except for the addition of water. It is made in one shot. This is considered the purest form of gin distillation, and one-shot London Dry Gin is considered by many to be the pinnacle of gin production and the essence of the master distiller's art. Sky Wave London Dry Gin made at the authors' Bucknell Distillery is made in this way.

Only 2 per cent of all gin produced in the world is made using the one-shot method, but it is often the preferred method of production for the craft distiller. Certainly, most start off using the method, even if they move to other approaches later. The difficulty, as well as the beauty, is that what goes into the still comes out of the still, and so your recipe has to be absolutely perfect because there can be no tinkering with flavours afterwards! You might be surprised to learn that some highly popular commercial brands such as Hendrick's and Martin Miller's are not London Dry Gins – check the label and see – because they could not achieve the flavours they wanted through distillation, and added flavour afterwards in various ways.

OTHER WAYS OR VARIATIONS OF PRODUCING GIN

Of course, there are other ways to produce gin, and we describe some of them here.

Cold Compounding

Cold compounding, as described in Chapter 2, is the process of gin production where the principal gin botanical flavours, including juniper, are imparted through maceration and not through distillation. The 'cold' comes from the fact that no heat is used, and the word is often dropped from the method description. A very old form of production, this is also a fine art as botanical quantities, as well as the length of time that they are steeped in the spirit, will influence the flavour. This type of gin produces a much oilier mouth feel, unless sophisticated filtration techniques are used (which also risks stripping flavour).

To make compounded gin, simply steep the botanicals in neutral spirit for a defined amount of time, filter and drink. The process really is that simple. Variations involve the ABV of the neutral spirit used (many people start out using vodka at 37.5 per cent ABV, but 50 per cent, or even 60 per cent, would absorb more botanical essential oils – then cut back to your serving ABV with water), the quantities of botanicals and the macerating time. This three-dimensional problem is at the heart, and the fun, of compounding.

Of course, some flavoured gins are produced by the sequence of distillation followed by compounding. For example, the fruity dry gins produced at the authors' distillery are made from distilled gin, which is then compounded with the fruit.

Old Tom Gin

Old Tom gin is a style rather than a production method, but it differs enough from the methods mentioned earlier to warrant discussion. Old Tom gin is any form of gin that is botanically intense, sugar sweetened, or botanically sweetened. This sweetening was originally introduced to mask the foul flavours produced by poor quality neutral spirit or poor ingredients. Very few modern Old Toms are made with pot still rough spirit (although some are); rather, they tend to be made with pure neutral spirit, so the flavour isn't particularly authentic. However, intense botanicals or sweetness, or both, mark an Old Tom. You may choose to design your gin this way, in which case you could legitimately call it an Old Tom.

Vapour Infusion

You may also hear or read of the term 'vapour infusion' in gin production – indeed, some producers trumpet this method on their labels. This term simply means that the botanicals are held in a gin basket, as already described, rather than in the wash in the still. Some producers believe that this method produces cleaner flavours, as the botanicals are not boiled. The flavours tend to be much subtler and less strong. A number of high-volume commercial gins, such as Bombay Sapphire, are produced this way. It also makes cleaning the stills considerably easier!

Grain to Glass

In your gin travels you may hear the phrase 'grain to glass', and the very few distilleries who achieve this claim that it is the nirvana of gin making. Again, very few *craft* distillers will achieve this, because it takes specialist equipment – but we discuss it here for completeness.

The neutral spirit used by the vast majority of gin distillers has been mentioned numerous times already, and is nearly always bought in from a commercial producer, even by the huge commercial gin distilleries. It is almost impossible to produce it on a smaller scale. The still for the process needs to be highly sophisticated, and has considerably more plates in the column than are usually used to distil the gin itself (upwards of twenty, as opposed to four to six), and so again is unlikely to be within the reach of the small craft distiller.

The process involves creating a 'beer' from the grain (or other agricultural product), which is distilled repeatedly – at least twice and often more – to produce extremely pure neutral spirit – and this purity is critical, or you'll be back to making Old Tom! The point is that the gin has been created from scratch from the grain, rather than buying it in. This is quite rightly a very proud claim made by those distilleries that achieve it.

Interestingly, some producers are using other agricultural products to produce the neutral spirit, not grain (such as grapes or potatoes), but grain remains the product used by most. Indeed, those who use other products claim it adds to the flavour – so one might ask the question whether it is truly 'neutral' – which, after all, is the meaning of the term.

The process of producing this neutral spirit can be fraught with difficulty and danger. The risk of explosion is very high if the process is not properly controlled (it produces highly flammable ethanol with very high concentrations of 90 per cent and upwards), the risk of producing highly poisonous methanol is also present, and of course all production must be recorded in detail and declared to HMRC, stating all alcohol produced, and ensuring that the appropriate duty is paid. Moreover, to be able legally to describe the gin made from this spirit as 'distilled gin' or London Dry Gin', the neutral spirit must be at 96 per cent ABV, and this is incredibly hard to achieve without industrial processes. It is for these reasons that most distilleries buy in their neutral spirit.

It is beyond the scope of this book to discuss its production in detail, and anyone attempting this is very strongly encouraged to obtain professional assistance and training before attempting it. It should *never* be done in a domestic setting.

Modern Technical Departures

Finally in this section we discuss more esoteric developments in gin production: ever more sophisticated methods of distillation are starting to appear, and to be used more and more frequently. Although initially at least these may be beyond the reach of the craft distiller, we mention two in particular for their technical interest.

The first is vacuum distillation. Some master distillers believe that certain botanicals, especially the citruses, are harmed by the relatively high temperatures in the still. They liken this to the difference in flavours between orange juice and marmalade, claiming that the heat can cause the citrus peels to caramelize and even burn. By reducing the air pressure in the 'still' (usually a rotary evaporator), vacuum distillation boils the alcohol at a much lower temperature, often room

The rotary evaporator (vacuum still) at the Twisting Spirits Distillery in Tewkesbury, Gloucestershire, England.

temperature, therefore not subjecting the botanicals to the usual extremes. The Twisting Spirits Distillery in Tewkesbury, Gloucestershire, uses this method as a part of its production process. Advocates claim a crisp, cleaner flavour.

The second relatively modern innovation involves distilling each botanical separately, then blending the resultant distillates in proportion to achieve the desired flavour profile. Distillers who use this technique claim that it again results in a cleaner taste, as the botanicals do not interfere with each other in distillation. It is also sometimes the approach used in gin-making experiences, where distillation itself is not offered. However, those who disapprove of this method claim that the interaction of the botanicals and essential oils in the distillation process itself has an influence on flavour, and this is lost by blended single distillations. Also, the jury is still out on whether the gin produced by this method can be styled 'London Dry'.

INDUSTRIAL PRODUCTION – THE CONCENTRATE METHOD

This chapter ends with a discussion of the way 98 per cent of gin in the world is produced: the concentrate method. It is used because it is a significantly more efficient way of distilling gin, and many claim that one cannot taste the difference between this and the one-shot method. Of course, purists claim that the one-shot method is the only true way. Note that the London Dry standard does allow the concentrate method to be used.

In this method, a multiple of the quantities of botanicals used for the one-shot method is added to the still. So for example, if 700g of juniper berries would normally be used in the wash, then perhaps four times this, 2.8kg, is added. This is repeated for all botanicals in the recipe, and then the gin is distilled as usual. The distillate will then be extremely rich in essential oils – four times as rich as the one-shot distillate. In fact it is far too rich to make finished gin; indeed, if it were cut with water at this stage it would immediately turn milky white as most of the oils would fall out of suspension: there would not be enough alcohol to hold them.

To bring the ratio of alcohol to oils back in line, the amount of actual alcohol in the distillate is calculated. This is relatively simple to do by knowing the quantity of distillate produced and the ABV of the distillate, measured using an alcoholmeter. Then, knowing this figure, the correct amount of neutral spirit is then added to the distillate – in this example, with four times the botanicals used in the wash, then three times as much alcohol in neutral spirit would be added in (with the actual amount being adjusted to take into account *its* ABV). Thus, including the alcohol already in the distillate, the correct ratio of alcohol to essential oils will have been achieved – in this case 4:4. This is often left to settle for a period, before cutting back with water as usual to bottling strength.

It can be seen therefore, that in this example, four times the quantity of finished gin has been produced for a single distillation, saving time and energy. It is significantly more efficient, which is why many mass producers use it. But it is not for the purists, and many craft gin distillers insist on the one-shot method, which guarantees that what goes into the still ends up in the bottle.

CHAPTER 4

THE COMPONENTS OF GIN

We have already learned that gin is a neutral spirit, infused with the essential oils of botanicals through the process of distillation or maceration. So, put simply, the components of gin are neutral spirit and botanicals. This chapter is about those key ingredients and how they are chosen and used. It also explores how their proportions can change the style of gin, and examines how modern, contemporary gins are starting to change the face and image of this quintessential spirit.

NEUTRAL SPIRIT

Before we rush headlong to the topic of botanicals, it is worth spending a little time considering one of the other key ingredients that goes into your still: the neutral spirit.

Neutral spirit is made from agricultural products such as grain, potatoes, apples, grapes, molasses – or even milk! By far the most common is grain, and the alcohol so produced is called 'neutral grain spirit' (NGS) or 'grain neutral spirit' (GNS). It is made by creating a 'beer' by adding water and yeast to the grains, then allowing it to ferment, which turns the sugars in the grain into alcohol. The alcohol level is very low at this point, only around 10 per cent, so it is then distilled repeatedly in highly specialized column stills until it is at 96 per cent ABV (alcohol by volume). It is extremely difficult, and certainly not worth the extra investment, to achieve greater than 96 per cent.

The purity of the neutral spirit is important for a number of reasons: in order to go on to use it to produce a London Dry Gin, by EU law it must be at 96 per cent; but also, the purer the spirit, the more neutral it will be. Spirits in the high 80 per cent or low 90 per cent ABV will retain some of the flavour of the original agricultural source, such as the grain, apples or grapes, and this will impart some flavour into the finished gin. Some producers, indeed, make a feature of this – but as a consequence use a different description for their gin than 'London Dry'.

Adding neutral spirit to the still. Neutral spirit is added to the wash with water to achieve a concentration of anything between 40 and 60 per cent ABV, depending on the distiller's preference and the recipe in use.

Most craft distilleries will buy in their neutral spirit. This image shows commercial 96 per cent pure neutral grain spirit (NGS). Strict handling rules apply, as in these concentrations it is highly flammable and dangerous to handle.

Even for NGS there can be some snobbery: many distilleries require a specific provenance – the authors' distillery, for example, insists on British-sourced grain spirit, whereas others might prefer grain spirit of eastern European origin (which, after all, is the home of vodka). Moreover, some distilleries make a point of producing their own neutral spirit (often termed 'grain-to-glass' or 'field-to-bottle') – this was explored briefly towards the end of Chapter 3.

Typically, a craft distiller will buy in their NGS from a commercial source. An internet search will reveal that a handful, and even some of the online drinks websites, such as Master of Malt, offer it in manageable quantities for those starting out. Be prepared for a shock, however: as this spirit is duty paid, and in reasonably high concentrations, it is expensive. As a rule of thumb, whatever the cost per litre (which in bulk can be around £5), expect to pay six times this (around £30) when the excise duty is added.

BOTANICALS

Clearly, the flavour of your gin comes almost entirely from the botanicals you choose to infuse into it. Remember that, for it to be a gin at all, the predominant botanical should be juniper; but outside this, the world is literally your oyster on the choice of botanicals. But first, what *is* a gin botanical exactly?

The European standard for distilled gin – and throughout the rest of this chapter, we assume you will be distilling – describes a botanical as 'any natural plant material'. That is, it must be naturally occurring, and it must have grown. This includes fruits, herbs, spices, seeds, roots and berries. They need not be specifically cultivated, hence the trend amongst some gin producers for using foraged botanicals. Some producers will use fresh or dried ingredients – that is, parts of the plant itself – whilst others may

Juniper berries growing on the bush. Technically they are not actually berries but rather fleshy conifer cones. The purple berries are mature, the green ones less so.

use flavouring, essences or tinctures derived from the plant.

Botanicals flavour your gin by transferring their essential oils into the liquid. The alcohol dissolves and suspends the oils. Different botanicals provide different densities and concentrations of oils, and this gives rise to the distinctive 'mouth feel' between gins.

The overwhelming influence on the flavour of your gin will be the botanicals you use, so you must choose them carefully. The difficulty – and the art – of how you impart the flavour of the botanicals into your gin is three-fold: first, botanicals don't always give the flavour you expect from their normal taste or smell when they are used in gin making; second, when in conjunction with other botanicals, they may alter their flavour again; and third, their contribution is not necessarily in proportion to the quantity used when in combination with other botanicals. This means that simply adding 10 per cent more of a botanical will certainly not just add 10 per cent more of the flavour of that botanical. The interactions and flavour combinations of botanicals comprise a complex mix that even scientists are currently struggling to unravel. Therefore, choosing which botanicals to use is worth long and careful consideration, and there will be a significant amount of trial and error involved before you reach that perfect recipe.

Coriander seeds are a common botanical in gin – almost as common as juniper. They add a hint of lemon spice and earthiness, and are used to give depth to a gin's flavour.

Adding juniper berries to the wash in the still. Some recipes may call for the botanicals to be steeped in the wash for a number of hours.

For these reasons it is recommended that your first gins use only a small number of botanicals as you experiment with the effect that they have, singly and in combination with each other. We recommend no more than five. Once you have achieved the effect you want with those, you can experiment by adding more botanicals one at a time, varying the amount until you arrive at the effect you want.

Designing Your Gin

The biggest mistake made by people new to gin making is to start by deciding which botanicals they want in their gin. This is simply the wrong way around. As we have said, botanicals may not deliver the flavours you expect, singly or in combination. Therefore, a better approach is to design the flavour profile of your gin completely divorced from the botanicals themselves, and then pick the botanicals to achieve that flavour profile. For example, you may decide you want your gin to be juniper heavy but with a mellow, floral depth.

Having designed your gin, you now set about finding botanicals that will deliver that profile. Juniper will always (must!) be the key ingredient, but by designing it to be juniper heavy you will use slightly more juniper berries than some lighter gins. Then you need to decide how to achieve the floral depth. You will research which botanicals achieve floral notes, and decide which, or which combination, to use. Once you have your basic recipe, the art is then to find the perfect combination of quantities, and this is where the trial and error in your recipes comes in – there is no exact science (or everyone would be doing it!).

Of course, the predominant flavour for gin must always be juniper, so this is where you must start. It is highly recommended that juniper comprises at least 50 per cent of your botanicals by weight to

Citrus botanicals are also very common in gins. Only the peel is used, fresh if possible, with as little of the pith as is achievable. The peel is where most of the essential oils are, as opposed to the fruit juices in the pulp of the fruit.

Botanicals Used in Gin Making

Botanical	Flavour Profile	Quantity for 2ltr of Wash
Juniper	The basic flavour of gin; depending on the source and quality, can give piney or fruity flavours	30g
Coriander	Brings a dryness; sometimes a spicy lemon effect	2g
Citrus peel	The peel is used, but not the flesh, as the peel is where most oils are	Small piece, around 1 × 1cm
Angelica root	Slightly floral but can be quite earthy or woody; important as helps bind other flavours to the gin	Powder, 1tsp
Rosemary	Herby	Use sparingly, can overpower; one small sprig will suffice
Basil	Herby aniseed	½ medium leaf
Various berries	Such as raspberries, elderberries, cranberries	Use sparingly, two or three depending on size; the sweetness comes through late
Apple	Very subtle apple flavours	1 thin slice
Sandalwood	Fragrant wood, informs the 'finish'	½ teaspoon
Nuts	Quite a variation of effects: experiment and see!	½ teaspoon
Vanilla	Strong vanilla, go easy!	3–4 seeds

avoid any challenge that you are not making gin. Use high quality juniper berries from a reputable source, and store them with care in a cool, dry environment – indeed, this applies to all your botanicals. Treat them with the respect they deserve, for they *are* your gin.

The table above lists some of the more traditional, and one or two unusual, botanicals used in gin making; it indicates what they bring to your flavour profile, and suggests some initial quantities for a small, 2ltr development still. It is deliberately varied, included not only to give you the base for your gin (juniper, coriander, angelica), but also to start you thinking about the wide variety of botanicals you might want to consider to achieve your profile.

As can be seen, gin botanicals can (and do) vary widely, and the limit really is only your imagination. There are very many websites describing others, and what flavour they impart. Guides on quantities to use are less freely available, and this is where you need to just give it a go. It is great fun to experiment with single botanicals to see what effect they have – but remember that effect may change in combination with others. As we have said, if this were easy, everybody would be doing it.

Every gin recipe needs a binding agent, used to 'bind' the flavours together and to the ethanol. Angelica root is one of the common botanicals to achieve this. It will also add an earthy, subtly floral flavour to the gin.

Maceration

We describe gin production step by step elsewhere, but maceration is a topic relevant here because it will influence the quantities of botanicals to use in your recipe.

Maceration is the term used when you soak some or all of your botanicals in the wash for a period before distillation. (It is also the process used in cold compounding, but that is a separate matter.) This steeping of the botanicals can release more of the essential oils than can be achieved just by distillation, and so some distillers use it as part of their process. It can therefore allow you to use lower quantities of ingredients and is therefore ultimately more economical. Note, however, that the additional essential oils released by steeping may result in a subtly different flavour, so to macerate or not to macerate is not a simple decision. Again, trial, error and experimentation are key to deciding whether you will or won't.

The Botanical Influence on Different Styles of Gin

Other than the way it is made (distillation versus cold compounding), the single biggest influence on the style of your gin is the choice and relative quantities of botanicals.

A classic, traditional gin is very juniper forward, meaning that the predominant flavour is juniper with all other botanicals providing the supporting cast. The skill here is to ensure that the non-juniper botanicals come through subtly, or provide depth and smoothness, without coming to the fore too much. If they do, you might be accused of creating a modern or contemporary gin.

A contemporary gin, or modern gin, is a spirit where juniper is still clearly in evidence, but other flavours such as citrus, spice and floral notes are more prominent than in a classic gin. These gins tend to be more complex and use more botanicals than classic gins, with intricate interactions between them. A gin, by definition, must use predominantly juniper (for which, read more than 50 per cent), but if the other botanicals are many and varied, the juniper-forward effect can be diluted to create a much more nuanced gin – a contemporary spirit.

Rose petals are a less common botanical but are still found in more floral gins. They can be quite strong, so use them sparingly.

Signature botanical gins are relatively self-explanatory. They are gins that deliberately bring a particular botanical or flavour to the fore, and they tend to state this. Juniper remains key, but the signature botanical sits alongside it with equal billing. All other botanicals are there only to add depth and smoothness. These gins tend to have relatively few botanicals. The skill is not to make the signature botanical too overpowering, nor drown out the juniper.

Finally, it is worth making a brief mention of navy-strength gin and botanicals. A navy, or navy-strength gin often has exactly the same botanicals as its lower ABV sibling but is bottled at 57 per cent or more. However, the interaction between the botanical essential oils and the alcohol is key here: the higher alcohol content will reduce the oiliness of the mouth feel, and the botanical oils will be released subtly differently on tasting. Different botanicals will react differently, so it is impossible to state a general rule; suffice to say a navy-strength version of a gin will feel, and taste, subtly different to its sibling – it is not just about strength.

Sourcing Botanicals

Finally we say a brief word about the sourcing and provenance of your botanicals: after all, juniper berries are just juniper berries – they're all the same, aren't they? Well, no.

Just as wine made from the same grape will vary widely from region to region and country to country, exactly the same applies to botanicals. Many botanicals are grown in a wide variety of countries and so naturally their flavour will change subtly. As your gin production grows, you may wish to explore different sources and suppliers of your raw ingredients. For example, juniper berries (of which there are a few types used in gin) are grown all over the world. In Europe, they are grown in some parts of the UK, around the Balkans, wider across Eastern Europe, in Italy and other mountainous countries bordering the Mediterranean. You might wish to experiment with which you prefer for your particular flavour profile. A fun way to do this is to explore the Origins series of gins, from Origin Gins at Atom Brands. These are gins distilled identically except for the source of juniper, and allow you really to taste the difference and choose which might work best for you.

Exactly the same approach applies to all your other botanicals, depending on the influence they have on your gin. For a signature botanical it is well worth investing in the time to find the source that is perfect for you, whilst a botanical that only adds depth or background might not be worth such investment, at first anyway.

There is also a considerable interest from consumers in knowing the provenance of your ingredients. For this reason, always ask your suppliers for as much information as you can about their sources. All ingredients should have a product data sheet, which you should ask for. In some cases, suppliers can tell you the individual producers of your ingredients; in others, especially where ingredients are blended from multiple sources, you may only be able to find the country of origin. Either way, be sure to enquire and have this information available. Some consumers also want organic ingredients, and so you may also wish to explore this approach; but remember, in order to describe your gin as organic, *all* its ingredients must be certified as such – including the neutral spirit.

Notwithstanding what we have said, initially – at least whilst you are developing your gin and experimenting with flavours – you will want a simple supply of botanicals, and the easiest way is to source them online. A quick internet search will provide you with a variety of suppliers. Some of the easiest to work with include JustIngredients and BuyWholeFoodsOnline, but many more are available.

CHAPTER 5

HOW TO MAKE GIN

This chapter offers a step-by-step guide to distilling your first batch of gin, using a still and the one-shot London Dry method – the true artisan gold standard. It focuses almost entirely on distillation, with only a small section at the end on cold compounding. This is because distillation is clearly the most complex approach.

To distil, it is assumed that you have a small still, around 2ltr in capacity, a heat source (if not integral to the still), and a supply of running water suitably plumbed into the condenser on your still – all as described in Chapter 2. It also assumes you have gathered the botanicals you wish to use, and have also sourced your base spirit, be it true neutral spirit or plain vodka. A typical set-up is shown in the picture.

A typical small still set-up, often of the type first used by new distillers. It is ideal for distilling tiny batches or for recipe experimentation. This is the author's development still, named 'Tilly' after their springer spaniel puppy.

RECORD KEEPING

It is important in everything you do that you keep thorough records. Use a notebook, your 'distiller's notebook', and write everything down. This is for two reasons: first, it is a requirement of your rectifier's and compounder's licences, and others, that you keep records of all of your use of alcohol and production of spirits; and second, you must be able to achieve consistency and repeatability, and recording everything you do will enable this.

If, for whatever reason, you decide to make a change to your process or ingredients, then record this as a change in your distiller's notebook. You need to be able to understand why an outcome was as it was, and record keeping will allow this analysis. It is easy to forget exactly what you did, so write it down in your notebook at the time.

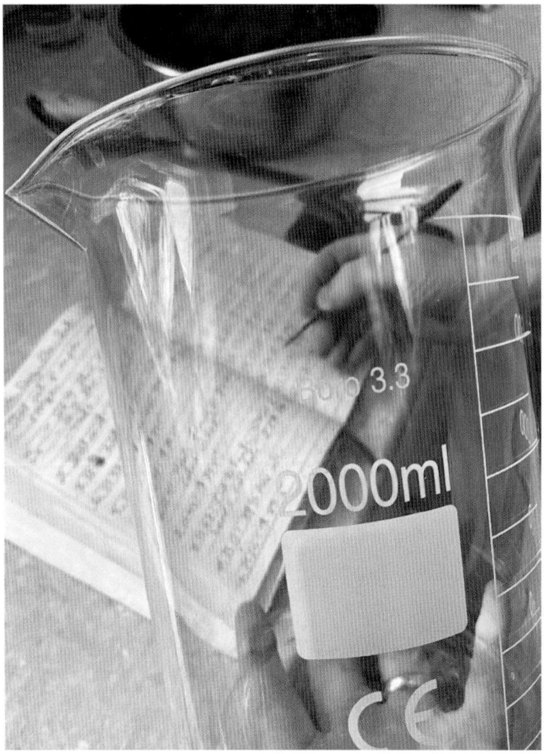

Making entries in the distiller's notebook. It is vital that a distiller makes a record of everything he or she does, for both accountability and repeatability purposes.

It is recommended that for every still run you record the following (the details of which will become clear in this chapter):

- The composition of the wash, including the volume of vodka or neutral sprit used and the water added
- The exact quantities of botanicals used
- The timings for the run:
  - when you turned on the still
  - when you cut the heads to the hearts
  - any changes you made to the wash temperature or thermostats
  - condenser water on and off
  - when you cut the hearts to the tails
  - the end of the still run
- Any changes to the process you may have made
- The volume of distillate produced
- The ABV of the distillate produced
- The volume and ABV of the cut gin produced

PREPARING YOUR STILL

Step 1: Preparing the Wash

The first thing you must do is to prepare the liquid for the wash at the correct ABV. For a 2ltr still we recommend an ABV of 38–40 per cent. This allows you to use either vodka or neutral spirit if you have sourced some. Once prepared it goes straight into the kettle of the still.

If you are using vodka, measure out about 1.8ltr (to leave room for botanicals) and add it straight to the still. No further preparation is necessary as it will already be at a suitable ABV – probably somewhere between 37 and 45 per cent (but check on the bottle). Then go to Step 2.

If you are using NGS, to prepare it you may need to 'cut' – that is, dilute – the neutral spirit down to 40 per cent ABV before adding it to the still. For example, if you have sourced neutral spirit at, say, 70 per cent ABV or more from online or specialist suppliers, then you need to add water to bring it down to 40 per cent ABV.

It is not difficult to calculate how much water to add. ABV is exactly what it says – alcohol by volume; so, if you have 1ltr of water at an ABV of 70 per cent, then

70 per cent of the volume is alcohol – that is, 700ml. This is known as 'actual alcohol', or 'absolute alcohol', abbreviated to AA. To cut this to 40 per cent, all that is necessary is to calculate how much liquid there would be if 700ml made up only 40 per cent of it. So, 700ml divided by 0.4 (that is, 40 per cent) gives 1,750ml. That is, we would need to make up the volume to 1,750ml so that the 700ml of AA was only 40 per cent of it – an ABV of 40 per cent. So, how much water do we actually add? Well, we had 1ltr (1,000ml) originally at 70 per cent ABV, so we need to add a further 750ml of water to make it 1,750ml at 40 per cent ABV.

If all this sounds a little daunting, there are a few very useful online calculators that distillers use; many use Distillique's. Here, use the blending tab and use the tool that suits you best. In fact, this is a great resource for all aspects of distilling, and it is worth a few minutes of exploration and getting used to what it offers.

The wash is prepared by mixing the exact amounts of neutral spirit and water to achieve the desired ABV. A distiller's calculator is used to work out the exact proportions.

People often ask what sort of water should be used in the wash. A few distillers insist on the same water they will use for cutting the distillate later on in the process, or they use extremely pure distilled water. In fact the former, if it has a heavy mineral content, can leave sludge deposits in the still, so is undesirable. In fact, nothing of the make-up of the water in the wash is carried over in the distillation (especially if you are using more complex equipment such as a thumper), so it is perfectly acceptable to use plain tap water in the wash in the still. Most distilleries will do this.

Step 2: Preparing and Adding the Botanicals

The next step is to prepare the botanicals. These should be weighed out to the gram, or measured precisely using measuring spoons. The key here is consistency and repeatability. Use a checklist and confirm that all are ticked off to make sure you haven't forgotten

Depending on the type of still used, botanicals may be added directly to the wash. Here, juniper is being added directly into the kettle of a small 2ltr still.

anything! Once your wash is ready, add the botanicals following the method you have chosen, either directly into the wash, or into a basket or other container in your set-up.

If you have chosen to macerate (steep) some or all of your botanicals, you will pause at this point for the length of time you have chosen. This can vary from a few hours to overnight. This step ends when all the botanicals have been left in place for the chosen amount of time in your process, and you are ready to distil.

Step 3: Distillation

Heating the Still

Once the still is prepared and contains the wash of alcohol and botanicals, it is ready for the heat source. An electric hotplate or element is best, as it is much easier to control, but some stills may be flame heated. Whichever approach you are using, start heating your still now.

An electric hotplate allows precise control of the heat input to the kettle. Here the control is set to maximum as the kettle is first heating up from cold.

The still will have a thermometer at the highest point. This is the key indicator for controlling your still. You are aiming for this to be kept at around 80°C; you will recall that alcohol boils at 78.3°C, so the top of the still needs to be above this temperature so that the alcohol doesn't recondense and run back into the wash – but not too high, so that any water vapour *does* recondense.

Depending on your heat source, it may take 20–30min for your still to reach temperature. When it approaches about 50°C, it is time to think about running the cold water through the condenser to cool it – you do not want distillate vapour coming all the way through the condenser, as it may cause the kettle to be under pressure, and the distillate and botanicals will

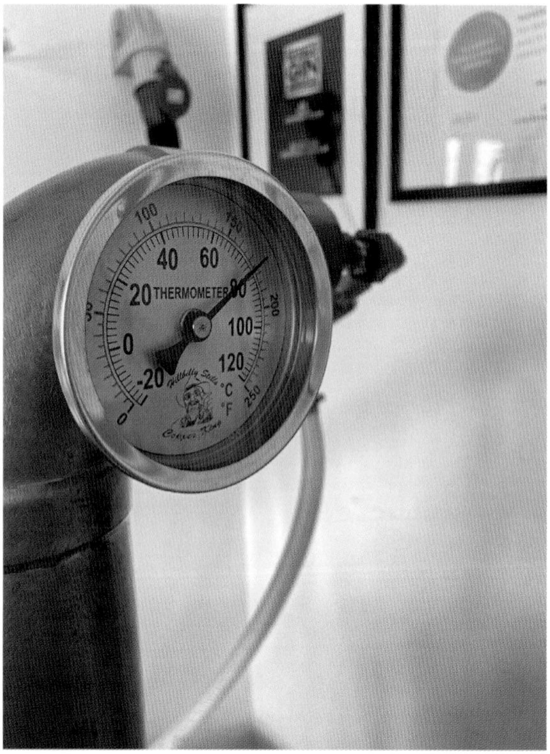

The column thermometer on a still is one of the most critical indicators for controlling the distillation process. It is this temperature (and not the temperature of the wash) that will dictate whether the distillate will rise over into the condenser, or reflux back into the kettle. Ideally the column would be kept at a temperature of about 80–81°C throughout the still run.

be forced through. It is important that the condenser is kept cool by the flowing water to cause the distillate to condense, and to ensure that no pressure can build up. You should constantly check that your condenser is cool throughout the still run, and adjust the water flow through it if necessary.

Once the still is at temperature, you may want to turn the heat source down; you now want to maintain the temperature at around 80°C, but you don't want it to get much hotter. Throughout the process, keep an eye on the thermometer and adjust the heat source as necessary. A hotplate with a thermostat is ideal for this.

Collecting the Distillate – the Spirit Run

You will have placed a suitable collecting beaker at the spirit outflow from the condenser when you set up your still. At about 30min after starting to heat the still, your distillate should start to flow into your collecting beaker. This is the start of the 'spirit run'. (Please note that all timings are extremely approximate and depend entirely on your set-up. In any case, your still should not be left unattended during a still run.) The distillate should be crystal clear and highly aromatic. At this stage in the run it will be at anywhere between 70 per cent and 85 per cent ABV, depending on the efficiency

Once the kettle, wash and column have reached temperature, and the condenser cooling water is flowing, the spirit will begin to flow through the outflow tube. It will flow slowly at first, building up to a steady trickle.

The distillate should be crystal clear. If it is not, something has gone wrong. Stop the still run and investigate.

of your still. The flow should be steady, but not too fast: the gentler the flow and the distillation, the smoother your end product will be, so don't rush it.

Cutting the Heads

In full-scale runs on large stills, especially where neutral spirit less pure than 96 per cent ABV has been used, then this part of the spirit run is collected as the 'heads'. Heads are collected, and usually discarded, for three main reasons: first, they can contain the undesirable bitter elements from the essential oils, which would impart a bad taste into your gin; second, this process helps to flush your still through from the previous run; but most importantly, the heads could contain highly poisonous methanol, which comes over in the earliest part of the distillation process. If you are using a base spirit of low purity, therefore, you should discard the first 100ml or so of the run. If, however, you are using highly pure ethanol or vodka, then there is no need to discard anything at this stage.

It should be noted that in the UK, ethanol must be highly diluted before it can be disposed of down domestic drains. So if you are discarding the heads, dilute them with tap water on a ratio of at least 10:1 before you pour them down the drain. (Please note that different laws may apply in different countries.)

However, assuming you have used highly pure ethanol or vodka in your wash, you are not going to discard any heads. Instead, you will keep even the first part of the spirit run and continue to collect the 'hearts'. If you are concerned about bitterness, it is worth considering that with a 2ltr still, the heads are so small in volume that it will not affect the flavour of your gin. But as you move to larger stills, you should indeed consider discarding some of the first distillate collected.

Collecting the Hearts

You will now run the still for anything up to 90min, possibly even longer. This is the stage of the process where you are collecting the spirit that will become your finished gin – the 'hearts'. This is the most flavoursome part of the run, avoiding the harshness and bitterness of the 'tails' at the end. Note that different flavours from the botanicals will come through at different stages of the run, with the lighter oils coming through earlier. Thus the aroma and flavour of your distillate will vary constantly, and this is perfectly normal and desirable.

Keep the temperature at around 80–85°C whilst maintaining a steady, gentle flow of distillate through the condenser. You may have to adjust your heat source regularly to achieve this. Remember: steady, gentle distillation will produce the best results.

Making the Cut to the Tails

When you have collected around 700ml of distillate you will be coming close to making the cut to the 'tails'. The tails are the bitter, heavy end of the spirit run, which you don't want in your finished gin as it will impart nasty flavours. Industrial and higher volume producers will decide when to make this cut by the alcohol content of the distillate stream. For example, their equipment will be constantly sensing it, and will automatically cut over to tails collection when the stream drops to 65 per cent ABV, or even lower.

Craft distillers, however, tend to want to make this decision themselves. After all, exactly when you make the cut can have a huge impact on the flavour of your finished gin: too early, and you are missing out on some of the delicious elements; too late, and that harshness and bitterness creeps in.

The easiest, and some craft distillers would say, the only way to decide, is by taste. With a little experience you will be able to *taste* the moment when the distillate goes from fruity and flavoursome, to bitter – and it can happen very quickly.

When you have collected about 700ml of distillate, take a small sample of the distillate stream in a shot glass, and taste it. If the taste is not bitter, keep collecting hearts. Repeat this every few minutes until you get the bitter taste. At this point, swap your collecting beaker for a different one to collect the tails. That's it – you've made the tails cut. As an upper bound, if you've collected more than about 790ml of hearts it is suggested that you have probably gone beyond the cut.

Run the still on to collect another 100ml or more, whilst keeping an eye on the temperature. Once it goes above 90°C there will be a high water content in your distillate and it is time to end the run. Turn off the heat source to the still, and after a few minutes, when the distillate has stopped flowing, turn off the water supply to the condenser.

When using a small development still, you will need to collect samples of distillate to measure the ABV, taste it, and decide on the appropriate points to cut to the tails.

The tails, unlike the heads, are not wasted. High in alcohol and essential oils, they can be reused in your next still run. It is traditional, and economical, therefore to add these tails into your still as part of the wash the next time you distil this recipe. It is not advisable to mix tails from different recipes, however – remember that the oils in these tails are specific to the botanicals used.

Step 4: Analysing Your Output

You now need to analyse, and record the details of, the distillate you have produced. You need to know two essential facts: how much distillate you have produced, and what its ABV is.

You can determine the volume by collecting it in a suitable volumetric beaker, with a certified scale marked on the side. Simply read off the volume from the scale, remembering to use the correct part of

The volume of distillate collected is read off on the scale of the measuring beaker, and recorded in the distiller's notebook.

The 'alcohol by volume' (ABV) content of the distillate and tails is measured using an alcoholmeter, and the results are recorded in the distiller's notebook. Here the reading for the tails is about 64 per cent ABV. Note that this may need to be corrected for temperature.

the meniscus, and ensuring your beaker is on a level surface. Record the volume of distillate produced in your distiller's notebook.

Next, to measure the ABV you will need a measuring jar, an alcoholmeter and a suitable thermometer. Take a sample of your distillate in the measuring jar and float the alcoholmeter in the sample. Read off the ABV from the alcoholmeter, again ensuring you use the meniscus correctly. The alcoholmeter will have come with instructions on how to do this. Ensure that you are indeed using an alcoholmeter (calibrated for ethanol) and not a hydrometer (calibrated for water), or your readings will be incorrect; some sold for beer and wine making are hydrometers, not alcoholmeters, so ensure you have the right type.

There is one further factor to consider: the temperature of the distillate at the moment of reading the ABV off the alcoholmeter. Alcoholmeters are usually calibrated to 20°C (except in Japan, where they are calibrated for 15°C). Check the instructions to confirm this. If your distillate is not at 20°C (it may be warmer if it has just come off the still), then the ABV given by the alcoholmeter may be slightly out and you may need to apply a correction. To do this, measure the temperature of your distillate with the thermometer, ensuring you leave the thermometer in long enough to give a stable reading. Then we can use a Distillique tool again to temperature correct the alcoholmeter reading. At the time of writing this is tool U9 under 'Unit Conversions'. Record the corrected ABV of your distillate in your distiller's notebook. You should also record the volume and ABV of tails collected.

Remember, measuring and recording the volume and ABV of your output is a legal requirement, and the

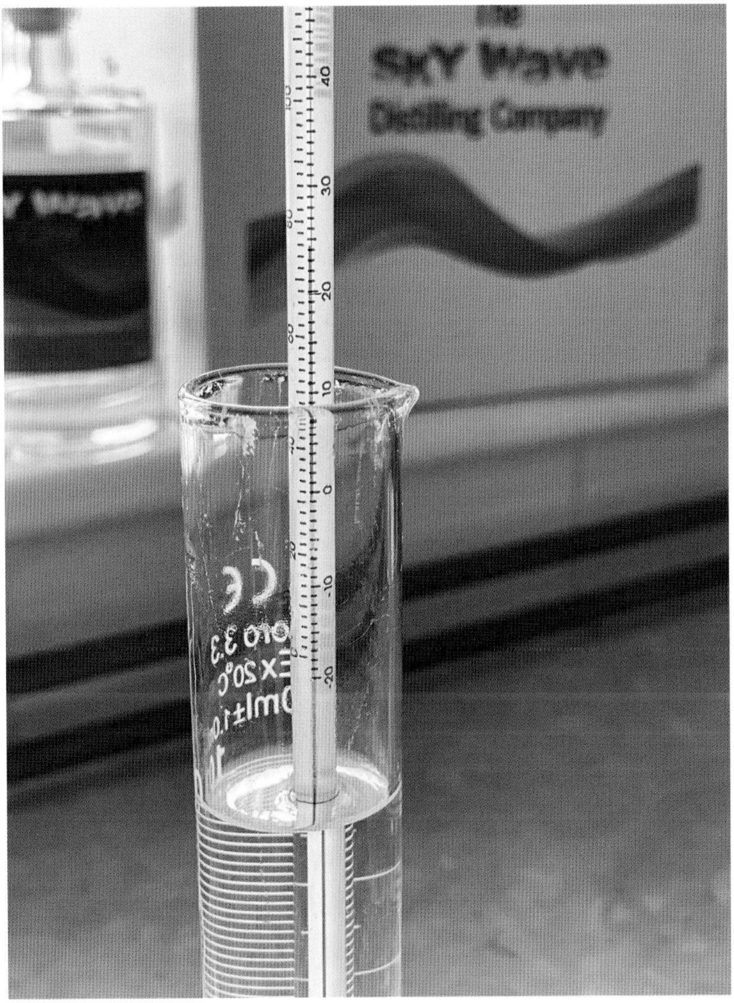

Alcoholmeters are usually calibrated to give correct readings for liquids at 20°C (15°C in Japan). If the liquid is at a different temperature, conversion charts or an online calculator must be used to correct the value. Here, a thermometer is being used to determine that the liquid is at 24.5°C, and so the alcoholmeter reading must be adjusted accordingly.

accuracy of your measurements is critical, especially if you intend to sell your gin.

Step 5: Cutting

The next step is to cut your gin to the ABV at which you will bottle it. It is accepted that the second use of the word 'cut', in a different context, is a little confusing here, but distillers use it for both meanings. In any case, it sounds much better than 'dilute', which has overtones of watering down – despite that being exactly what you are going to do!

It is at this point that the quality of the water is absolutely critical. Unlike for the wash, the water you use here will directly affect the taste of your gin. It is therefore important that you choose wisely. Start off with a water you like (or just use distilled water, which will be flavourless), try it, and see whether it complements your gin. At the authors' distillery we use a local natural mineral water that works perfectly with our gin.

Your next decision is at what ABV you wish to serve your gin. Commercial gins go as low as 37.5 per cent (which, of course, is the legal minimum for a London Dry Gin), which maximizes profit as it contains less gin and more water. Craft gins tend to be higher than this, in the low or even mid 40s. But it is not just about profit margins. The ABV at which you choose to bottle makes two notable differences to your gin, other than the obvious effect on alcoholic strength. First, it can affect the 'mouth feel' – how rich, oily or viscous your gin feels in the mouth. Second, it can affect the flavour itself absolutely. Both of these are because there are simply more of the botanical essential oils by volume. The perfect ABV of your gin is more than just a number, and again is worth a little trial and error.

Calculating how much water to add to achieve that ABV is similar to the calculation done in 'Preparing the Wash' above. You know how much distillate you have and its ABV, and therefore you can calculate how much 'absolute alcohol' is in your distillate, and thus how much water to add. But again, if you don't fancy this, Distillique comes to the rescue. In this case, at the time of writing, use tool B1 under 'Blending'.

Once you have added the water you have finally made gin, but it must be allowed to rest to allow the blending to take place. Some master distillers believe that you need seven days or more for the magic to happen. Indeed, a chemical process takes place when you add the water, and this does take time: the water and ethanol molecules bond, which gives off a small amount of heat – enough that you can feel it in your mixing jar a few minutes after adding the water. Interestingly, the total volume of liquid also reduces slightly. If, say (using easy numbers), you add 500ml of water to 1,000ml of distillate, you do not get 1,500ml of gin. Depending on the ABV of the distillate, you actually get about 1,480ml! Although scientists don't fully understand why, they believe it is because, as the water molecules bond with the ethanol molecules, they actually partially bond inside each other's structures and so reduce the overall volume slightly.

Also, if you are cutting with water that has a very heavy mineral content, this may fall out of solution when mixed with the distillate. Any solution can only hold so much soluble matter, and with the botanical oils being lighter than minerals, they tend to be held in the solution whilst shedding the heavier minerals. Thus, you may get mineral sediment settling on the bottom and sides of the mixing vessel. It is better that this sediment is allowed to settle out at this stage, rather than in the bottles, so this is another reason to allow the gin to rest.

It is clear, therefore, that you must rest the cut gin for a period of time before doing anything else with it. Do not make any rushed decisions on changing recipes or altering cutting ratios until it has suitably rested. Flavour can change quite noticeably during this period. Only after the resting period should you think about bottling.

Distilled, spring or mineral water is added to the distillate (known as 'cutting') to bring the gin down to bottling strength. This process is a chemical reaction that can cause a little agitation, and which gives off a small amount of heat as the water and ethanol molecules rearrange and bond.

Once your gin is rested it is worth checking the ABV again to make sure you made your calculations correctly. The gin can be adjusted if necessary at this point and allowed to rest further. You will, of course, retest the ABV again before bottling, because to bottle at a different ABV from that stated on your label is a criminal offence!

Step 6: Clearing Down

Once the still has cooled down, you will need to clean it out. That is relatively easy for a 2ltr still. Drain off the liquid, dilute it at least 10:1 with water (it still contains some alcohol) and dispose of it down the drain. Put the botanicals into compost. Wash the still in warm water, ensuring that all botanicals have been removed, and allow to dry, not forgetting to run the lyne arm and condenser through with water.

Ensure the tails are suitably bottled, ready to use in your next still run.

DOs AND DON'Ts

We have given a comprehensive description of how to use a 2ltr still to distil your first batch of gin, but it is worth re-emphasizing some key dos and don'ts.

Do:

- Keep detailed records in your distiller's notebook of everything you do
- Calculate your wash ABV properly. Use an online calculator if you are not comfortable with the maths
- Weigh or measure your botanicals precisely according to your recipe. Consistency and repeatability are key
- Keep an eye on the still column temperature, and maintain it at about 80°C
- Maintain a steady, not too fast, flow of distillate
- Learn how and when to make your tails cut, whether by taste or volume collected
- Collect and reuse your tails
- Calculate and record the volume and ABV of the distillate produced
- Calculate and record the volume and ABV of the tails collected

Don't:

- Worry about using a particular water in your wash. It makes no difference
- Forget to turn on your condenser cooling water!
- Use an alcoholmeter without correcting for temperature
- Forget to turn off the condenser cooling water at the end of the run
- Even think of pouring heads or liquid waste into the drain unless it is heavily diluted, at least 10:1
- Think you have finished the job until your still is immaculately cleaned

COLD COMPOUNDING

Everything so far in this chapter has been about *distilling* your gin, but as we have discussed, cold compounding is an equally valid and historical method of production. It is called 'cold' compounding as no heat is used in the production of the gin. Of course, it is not distilled at all: rather, the botanicals are soaked in the vodka or neutral spirit for a period of time to extract their oils. Some very fine craft and commercial gins are made in this way. It is a simpler process and needs very little equipment, and so is often preferred as a first foray into craft gin making. That said, whilst the process is simpler, it could be argued that the *craft* is harder, as some say it is far more difficult – and time consuming – to perfect a recipe.

To make compound gin, gather together the tools and ingredients described in Chapter 2, and follow these steps:

Steps 1 and 2: Preparing the Wash, and Preparing and Adding the Botanicals

These steps are identical to the steps in distillation. You still need to prepare your wash and botanicals, and then add the botanicals to the wash.

There are two main differences in preparing the wash. First, often the ABV at which you will serve your gin is decided at this stage, and the wash cut accordingly. It is, of course, possible to add more neutral spirit afterwards (to raise the ABV), or water (to lower it), but it is easier to set the ABV now than to adjust it later. Either way, record the ABV in your distiller's notebook. Second, the water you use now is very important, as it is the water you taste, so again, you should choose your water with care.

There is also a significant difference in preparing the botanicals. The process of distillation extracts much more of the essential oils than compounding, therefore you need to use greater quantities to achieve the same effect. There is no simple formula here, as different botanicals react in different ways to soaking – some give up their oil more easily than others. For anything powdered, you can use about the same quantities. Anything dried needs about half again, as do berries and fresh leaves – but that is absolutely not a guarantee for any given botanical. Like much of gin making, you will need to experiment with your recipe and see what happens.

Step 3: Maceration

In this step, you simply allow the botanicals to soak in the wash. How long you soak them is again part of the art, but it is worth leaving them for at least fourteen days, and some recipes call for a month; but if the botanicals haven't given up their oils by then, they are not likely to. Store the wash in a sealed container in a cool dark place, and agitate it daily. It is this waiting that makes experimentation with compounding such a lengthy process, and therefore the creation of a compounded gin such a difficult art.

In cold compounding, the botanicals are macerated, or steeped, in the wash for a period of time. Some botanicals float, so it is important to stir the wash regularly to encourage as much of the oil content as possible to be dissolved by the ethanol.

Step 4: Filtration

After the period of maceration your gin is effectively ready. You will need to filter it at this point using as fine a filter as you can. Despite this, unless you're using a professional filtration system, it is likely that the gin will still be slightly yellowy brown. This is unavoidable and doesn't affect the taste. Once you've filtered it as finely as you can, you should again confirm the ABV and adjust it if necessary. It is also worth mentioning that the mouth feel of compounded gins is often much more unctuous and oily as a result of the process.

You could attempt to filter it further by using a method called cold filtration. To do this, place the gin in suitable containers in the freezer. After twenty-four hours it will not have frozen but will be thicker and more viscous. If you again filter it at this point, using as fine a filtration system as you can, you will remove more of the fine particles and this may make the gin clearer.

SUMMARY

In this chapter we have described the detailed steps for producing gin, using both distillation and cold compounding. We have also highlighted some 'dos and don'ts' for distilling. Throughout, we have stressed the need for adequate record keeping. Not only is this a legal requirement, but the key to success in the art of creating a fabulous gin is experimentation, and you can only experiment successfully if you keep a strict record of what you've done, and thus know what to change.

CHAPTER 6

FILTRATION, BOTTLING, SEALING AND LABELLING

Once you have produced your fabulous gin, you will want to present it in the best possible light. If your gin is just for friends and family, you may accept a lower standard of presentation: home filtration and home-made labels may suffice and add charm to your offering. However, this will not be enough for commercial production. This chapter explores topics concerning filtration, bottling, sealing and labelling your product to give it that professional feel.

FILTRATION

The Importance of Filtration

No matter how much care and effort you put into the process of producing gin, nor how hygienic your facilities and apparatus are, at some point something may get into it, be it dust, a hair or other airborne matter. This is because in craft gin making in particular, containers are often open to the air whilst, for example, distillate is collected. We have seen that in a typical set-up, distillate flows from the condenser or the parrot outlet into a collecting vessel, and it would be easy for something to enter the process here, for instance. For this reason it is absolutely vital that appropriate filtration is used at the point of bottling to ensure that the contents of the bottles are fit for human consumption.

If you are using the cold compounding method of production, filtration is equally important as you need to remove not only the botanicals themselves from the wash at the end of the maceration period, but also the fine particles left behind. In addition it may be desirable to filter even further to achieve as clear a gin as possible.

Types of Filter

Filtration is the process of passing the gin through some form of medium that allows the liquid (including the botanical essential oils) to pass through, whilst trapping any undesirable solid matter. Filtration can be achieved in a number of ways, depending on your

Examples of filter types: filter paper, a washable filter, and professional filter cartridges. The type of filtration you choose to use will depend on many factors, including whether you intend to offer your gin for sale commercially.

set-up and how complex and professional you need to be. At one end of the scale you may choose to use filter papers (either coffee filters or more professional papers) or washable domestic filters, while at the other you might wish to use professional in-line filters as part of the bottling process. Whichever you choose to use, it is important to understand some characteristics of the filtration processes to ensure you have used the appropriate equipment and technique.

Particle Size

Filters will specify the smallest particle size they are able to trap: for example, a filter may be described as a '1 micron' filter. This means that it will trap particles with a dimension of 1 micrometre and above, but smaller particles will pass through. Typically, a straining bag may be 50–75 micron, and a washable coffee machine-type filter will be rated at 10–15 micron. Filter papers are commercially available rated 7–10 micron and are often sold specifically for wine and spirits filtration. Professional filters will achieve 5 micron, 1 micron and 0.5 micron or even less.

For coarse filtration of compound gins, and other processes such as adding fruit to flavour a gin, it is recommended that a coarse filter bag is used initially to remove the visible physical particles. This will help to prevent finer filters from clogging quickly.

It may then be desirable to filter fruit gins down to around only 5 micron. This is because some of the flavour will come from particulates. 5 micron will be sufficient to remove any spurious matter, but leave in fruit particles for flavour. Note that if filtering at 5 micron, a small amount of sediment may form on the bottom of bottles, but this should be acceptable if you are using fresh fruit.

For compound gins, in order to achieve as clear a final product as possible you should filter at 0.5 micron or less. Much of the cloudiness and colour comes from very fine particles, which you may want to remove. However, this is a balance between flavour and mouth feel on the one hand, and the attractiveness of a clear gin on the other, so you may wish to experiment to find the optimum process for your gin.

For a distilled gin, all the flavour and oils should be in solution, and so filtering at 0.5 micron or finer (0.2 micron) should be the norm.

Coarse filtering fruit from a fruit gin prior to finer filtration. This removes the larger pieces and helps to prevent subsequent finer filtration from clogging.

Cold Filtration

If you really want to achieve the finest filtration possible, choose the lowest rated filter you can find, and use the process of cold filtration. This involves putting your gin in a freezer for a few hours until it is at as low a temperature as you can get it. It won't freeze, because ethanol freezes at –114°C, but it will turn a little thicker and more syrupy as the water molecules and oils start to approach solidity. In this state, although not necessarily visible, crystals start to form around any particles present, which makes trapping them in filtration more likely.

Filter the liquid when it is as cold as possible to remove maximum particulates, and you may find that even compound gin can be made clear – especially if the process is repeated a number of times.

Many commercial gins use this process for a crystal-clear final product, and some use it to remove the louche present in their gin from the abundance of botanical oils. However, craft distillers generally tend to eschew the process as it can remove mouth feel and flavour by actually filtering out some of the very oils you have worked so hard to distil into your gin. Again, it comes down entirely to personal preference and trial and error to discover exactly what works for your gin.

BOTTLING

At first, bottling can seem fun and even quirky. You might use a conical filter and funnel to fill each bottle by hand, and even make a virtue of it to your customers. But after fifty bottles the novelty soon wears off, and after a thousand you may wonder why you started doing it this way at all!

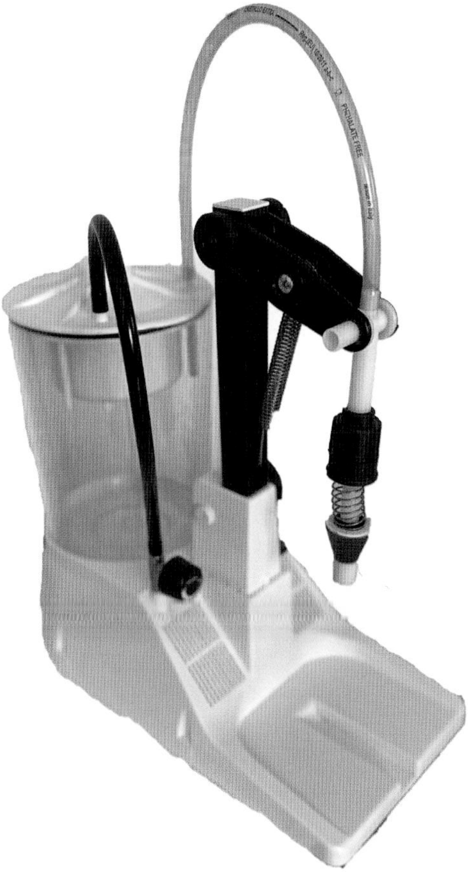

An Enolmatic single-bottle vacuum bottle-filling machine. This machine is manufactured by Italian company Tenco, and can be fitted with heads for miniature and smaller bottles.

Moreover, it is vital for Trading Standards purposes that you are absolutely sure that you have filled every bottle absolutely to the volume you claim (or to an average value of that volume if you are marking your labels appropriately with the 'e' symbol). To achieve this, one of two methods can be used.

The more difficult and time consuming, but the more precise method, is to use a stamped, certified, volumetric measure. In the UK, these are certified beakers bearing a government stamp (much like a pint glass in a pub), stating that the volume markings are correct. Accurately using such a measure ensures that every bottle is filled sufficiently – and one tends to go slightly over just to be sure. However, measuring out every bottle in this way soon becomes impractical, so another approach is used by almost all craft distilleries.

This second method relies on the fact that all commercial bottle specifications will state a 'fill line', above which the bottle is filled to its nominal volume. By setting equipment designed for this purpose to fill to that level (or slightly over), it is certain that the bottle has been filled sufficiently. Most craft distilleries will use vacuum fillers, which create a vacuum in the bottle that sucks the liquid in, until the level of the liquid itself seals the vacuum tube and this cuts off

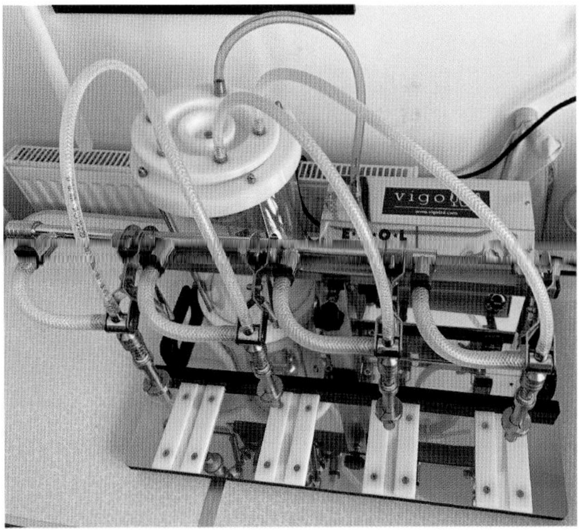

An Enolmaster four-bottle vacuum bottle-filling machine. These machines are used in craft distilleries across Europe. A skilled operator can fill more than 600 bottles an hour.

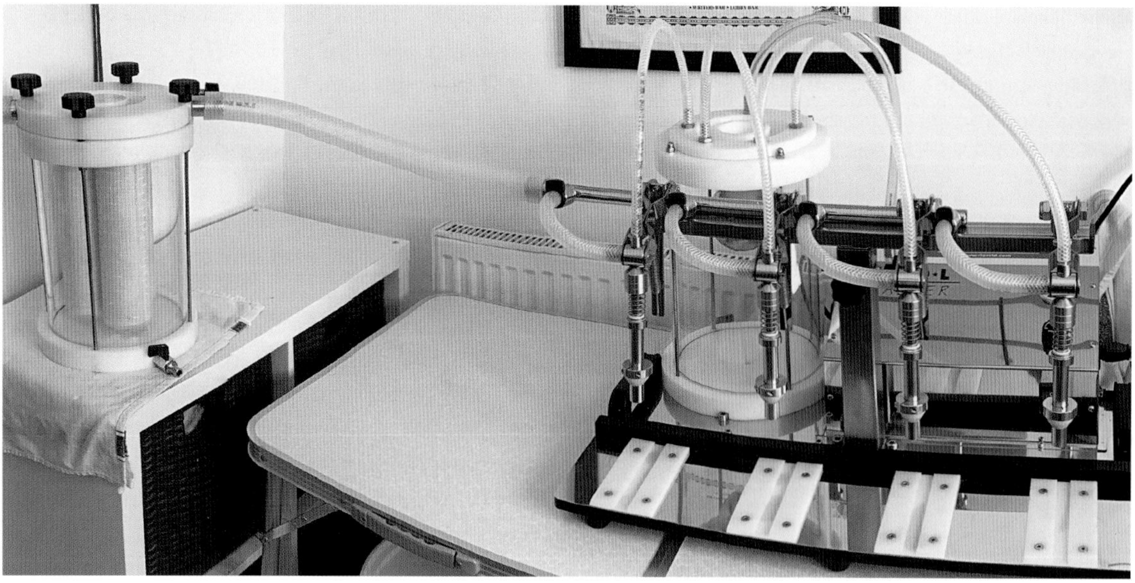

The Enolmaster four-bottle vacuum bottle-filling machine with in-line filtration at the authors' distillery. This machine is used, with varying filters and heads, to bottle all the distillery's products.

the flow. Setting this level correctly ensures that each bottle is filled to the perfect level time after time. Such machines are available relatively cheaply in single- and four-bottle versions, with larger industrial machines obviously also available.

There is a third method, rarely used by craft distilleries (because it involves extra equipment, multiple steps and density calculations), but described here for completeness. This method uses the weight of the liquid in the bottle. The bottle being filled sits on a weighing scale, which is an integral part of the machine. When the scale determines that the correct weight has been reached, it turns off the filler valve electronically.

All these systems allow in-line filtration, ensuring that filtration is achieved at the moment that liquid is bottled, removing almost all chance of contamination.

All bottles should, of course, be thoroughly washed and rinsed before filling in order to remove any packaging or storage debris that may have entered the bottle. Unlike beer brewing and wine making, however, as long as bottles have been kept in clean and hygienic conditions, they do not need to be sterilized before filling.

SEALING

All bottles must be sealed in some way, to prove to the consumer that they haven't been tampered with. There is a wide variety of seals, but they come in three main categories: which you choose depends on your branding and the aesthetic you wish to achieve.

The first and probably the easiest method is to apply a simple sealing strip (sometimes called a tamper strip) across the stopper and down the sides of the neck of the bottle. This also offers an opportunity for more branding.

The second approach, which requires a little more equipment but can give a very premium look, is wax sealing. Specially made sealing wax is heated to liquid state, and the bottles are dipped upside down in the liquid wax. The wax soon cools, giving a perfect seal. The difficulty of this approach is that it is difficult for the consumer to remove the wax unless a tear strip is embedded, and this can be difficult to apply at the point of dipping in the wax.

The third approach is to use shrink capsules. These are PET or PVC capsules, which are placed over the stopper and neck of the bottle. When heat is applied,

Bombay Sapphire bottles showing their branded tamper-evident sealing strips over their stoppers.

A typical gin bottle showing a wax seal, created by dipping the inverted bottle into molten wax.

A typical gin bottle showing the 'shrink capsule' approach to sealing. The capsules are placed on the head and neck of the bottle and shrunk into place using heat.

using a heat gun or bespoke tool, the capsule shrinks into place forming a tight fit and tamper-evident seal around the head of the bottle. These can be applied very quickly, and a wide variety of colours – or even bespoke branding – is readily available. They are usually made with a tear strip for easy removal.

LABELLING

Labelling by hand is also one of those processes that is enjoyable, briefly, at first, but soon pales. Labelling by hand without any form of machine is extremely time consuming, and can be the bottleneck to the whole production process. Automatic labelling machines are, of course, available, but tend to be large and expensive. For this reason, most craft distilleries, at first at least, will use a manual labelling machine to make the process more efficient. Manual machines also enable much more precise placement of labels compared to applying them purely by hand and eye, thus giving a more professional finish.

Most manual machines involve ensuring that the labels are wound on a spool ready for application. The bottle is placed in position, and the label is applied by manually winding a handle, which simultaneously feeds the label and turns the bottle. Semi-automatic machines are also available, which start as soon as the bottle is placed in position, and are powered by a

A manual labelling machine. Labels are applied by placing the bottle in position as shown and turning the handle.

motor that replaces the manual handle. Some of these machines can also apply text to the labels as they pass, allowing, for example, batch numbers to be applied.

It should be noted that all these machines require the bottles to be round in shape. Square or non-uniform shapes are extremely problematic for labelling unless bespoke machinery is used, and so it is highly recommended that craft distilleries consider this point when choosing their bottle shapes as part of their branding. It is also worth noting that when labels are produced it is important that they are wound on the spool appropriately. The label proof from the label printer should say something like 'Outside Wound Left Edge Leading', which means that the labels are on the outside (top) of the backing sheet, and that they will flow with the left edge first. This allows them to be applied on to a rotating bottle. Avoid the top or bottom edge leading, as these cannot be applied by a machine that rotates a bottle as it applies them.

CHAPTER 7

FLAVOURED GINS

WHY FLAVOUR GINS?

Gin has always been flavoured, but not in the sense that we know it now. A London Dry Gin today will take its flavour from the botanicals with which it is distilled, and nothing but water can be added after distillation, in line with the strict adherence to the London Dry method of production. But back in the seventeenth and eighteenth centuries, gin was not produced in such a sophisticated manner. In fact much of London's gin was made in the myriad residential houses, which began production to fuel the gin craze, using pot stills that created a rougher version of what is now recognized as gin. In 1726 there were estimated to be 1,500 residential stills in London.

At this time it is said that gin was sometimes flavoured with turpentine to create woody notes to accompany the taste of juniper. But in reality it is more likely that the addition of turpentine, and even sulphuric acid, was not to help with flavour but to aid unscrupulous distillers in making their gin go further. However, on the whole gins produced in the 1700s were much less refined and delicate than the gin we are used to today. Often flavouring was used to disguise the rather unpleasant taste and make it more palatable. Liquorice or sugar were sometimes used to make the cheap drink more appealing to an insatiable drinking public.

The eighteenth century gave rise to a style of gin referred to as 'Old Tom', a softer, sweeter style of gin, often containing sugar. It was drier than the Dutch Genever and sweeter than the London Dry. It was created as an antidote to the harsh pot-still gins in a time before the invention of the column, which nowadays some distillers like to use to produce smooth, complex gins. Old Tom gin was popular for decades, but eventually technology improved, leading to better methods of distilling, and there was less need to find ways to disguise the base alcohol by adding sweetening agents or huge amounts of botanicals.

The curiosity for every type of gin imaginable has driven modern distillers to revisit the heritage drinks of the past. Old Toms, which are often sweeter, have been recreated for the modern drinker.

The sweeter Old Tom version of gin was beginning to lose its following by the 1940s, and the downward spiral continued until the 1970s, when it had virtually disappeared. Tastes had changed, and as the distillation of gin became more sophisticated and consequently smoother, so the taste moved towards a drier gin. But with the gin boom in the late noughties, the curiosity for every type of gin imaginable drove distillers to revisit the heritage drinks of the past. So it has come to pass that a number of Old Toms have been recreated for the modern drinker, some of whom actively prefer a sweeter gin, some reinvested with new flavours for today's drinkers.

Creating Difference

In traditional gin, botanicals such as juniper, coriander seed, cardamom and fruit peels are added to base alcohol, and their oils are extracted during distillation to create a typically dry, spicy and citrusy spirit. In fruit-flavoured gins, sugar and fruit flavours – occasionally derived from whole fruits such as raspberries, strawberries, cherries or rhubarb, but more often from cheaper concentrates, essences and flavouring agents – are also added, usually after distillation, to create a far sweeter drink. In fact, it's true to say that many flavoured gins on the market today are actually liqueurs with lower levels of ABV (alcohol by volume) than the 37.5 per cent ABV minimum required to be called a gin, and with varying amounts of sugar, flavours and colours added to them.

The range of flavoured gins has led to the consumption of gin rising by 751 per cent in 2018. It has certainly helped to boost sales. According to the Wine and Spirits Trade Association, gin sales reached £1.9 billion in the UK in 2018. One of the factors helping with the growth in gin sales is the wide variety of

The rise in fruit-flavoured gins has led to many different flavours being created, either from whole fruits, such as blackberries, or more often using cheaper fruit flavourings.

In 2018, 1.6 million additional shoppers chose to buy a bottle of flavoured gin. Many were attracted by the wide range of original flavours now available, such as lavender gin.

flavoured gins that are now available. In 2018, the trade publication *The Grocer* reported that 1.6 million additional shoppers chose to buy a bottle of flavoured gin. The choice of broader flavoured gins has, in turn, opened up a whole new market of 'non' gin drinkers, who find they are attracted to the once unfashionable drink by the new flavours, usually because they are sweeter.

So for non-gin drinkers and gin fans alike there is now a huge range of flavours covering everything imaginable from Christmas pudding to spit-roasted pineapple gin. There seem to be no boundaries to what can be added to gin nowadays in the search for the next new and novel offering for an eager gin-drinking crowd. A Parma violet gin, for example, with a hue to match, can be seen being mixed up with real Parma violet sweets by bartenders as part of a somewhat sickly offering but devoured by many in pubs up and down the country, images of which are splashed across many an Instagram account on a Saturday night.

Many non-gin drinkers have been drawn to the gin offering due to the surge in creative and enticing new flavours, including seasonal ones such as Christmas pudding-flavoured gin.

THE TONIC QUESTION

As an interesting aside, people who say they don't like gin are usually mistaken. Very often it is actually the bitterness of the tonic they dislike. After all, most gins are traditionally served with a quinine-flavour tonic. It is well known that British sailors in the eighteenth century, bound for exotic lands, were issued with quinine to fight illness. They so disliked its bitter taste that they mixed it with tonic to disguise it. As all sailors were also issued with regular measures of gin, they would mix that into the tonic to disguise further the taste – and hence the 'gin and tonic' was born.

Flavoured gins have also been inspired by retro flavours appealing to drinkers' childhoods, such as Parma violet gin, which is often served with actual Parma violet sweets as a garnish.

The explosion of flavours can sometimes result in the gin bar at a pub looking very colourful and also very appealing to new gin drinkers, such as this bar at The White Horse in Kings Sutton, Oxfordshire.

It has led to some viewing the divergence of the market as not necessarily good news for distillers. The explosion in the flavoured gin market can be compared to a similar craze when flavoured vodkas flooded the market in the 1990s. For some, when flavours start to dominate a spirit, it is a warning bell, a signal that the beginning of a decline in the gin craze might be in sight. Distillers need to be on their guard not to dilute or lessen their brand by releasing many different flavours. Their range, a little like the bars of many a British pub these days, can end up looking like a colourful and very enticing sweet shop.

Different Flavours

The breadth and depth of ingredients available to flavour gin is as long as a piece of string. Historically, as discussed earlier in this chapter, gin was sweetened with sugar to try to mask the unpalatable taste of cheap, rough gin knocked out in a poor still using cheap or inferior ingredients. However, now there are gin makers who use everything from Earl Grey tea to pomegranate to add a distinct flavour to their tipple. The flavoured gin market has taken over where the flavoured vodka market left off. The most popular flavours tend to be fruity or floral ones, but one company even created a gin that tried to reflect the smells and flavours of having a barbecue on a British beach!

CREATING FLAVOURED GIN

Creating a flavoured gin can be done in two ways. There is the home infusion method, in which no gin is actually created, but rather a shop gin is used, and then fruit or other flavourings are added and left to steep until ready, which can be a number of days or weeks.

Sometimes sugar is also added to achieve the desired sweetness.

The second method for creating flavoured gins is the professional route. First of all the gin is distilled from scratch, then selected fruits, herbs and spices carefully added and left to macerate. When the gin maceration period ends, a professional fruit press extracts the juice before it is filtered through a bottling plant into bottles.

Let's take a look at the home infusion method first of all.

When choosing home infusion, consider the type of gin that will be used as the base. The more neutral the gin, the more the flavours of the infused fruit will be dominant in the final product.

Home Infusion

There are many sites on the internet offering to help keen gin drinkers flavour their own gin. Most are done on a very small scale of, say, 1 or 2ltr at a time, and just for domestic consumption. The following section describes a simple method for home infusion.

Choose your gin: Try and choose the best quality gin you can afford if you are not using one you have distilled yourself. As in all aspects of food and drink, the better quality the base gin, the finer the results that can be expected. If you choose a clean-tasting, uncomplicated gin, such as a neutral-style London Dry, then the infusing flavours may come through more strongly. However, a complex gin could complement some of the more subtle flavours added, and would create something unusual and unexpected as a result. To a certain degree there is some experimentation to be had here.

Creating a gin infused with fruit such as raspberries is relatively straightforward and can be done with limited equipment such as a large jar and a bottle into which to transfer the gin when it is ready to drink.

Choose your flavours: Gin traditionally contains juniper, coriander and cardamom among its botanicals, so choose a flavour to complement the natural elements of this glorious tipple.

It's great to use seasonal flavours, so keep your eyes on the hedgerows for berries, elderflowers and herbs that you could use. Alternatively, choose flavours that have wide-ranging appeal, such as citrus fruits. Here are some suggestions to get you started:

Fruit: raspberries, blackcurrants, blueberries, oranges, apples
Vegetables: rhubarb, chilli, celery

Herbs and plants: rosemary, thyme, lavender, mint, elderflower – though be careful to get the right type of elderflower, as there are two common varieties in Britain. Using the wrong one will lead to a Kilner jar full of an alcohol smelling and looking like cat urine!

Remember, the more you use, the stronger the flavour. Use around 200–400g of fruit per litre of spirit.

The bottling technique: Add your spirit to a Kilner jar or some other sealable container. Make sure the kit is clean and sterile to avoid the spirit going bad. Then add the infusing ingredient. If you wish to add sugar you can do so now, although it will mean that, strictly speaking, you are creating a liqueur. Remember that as a rule you add half the weight of sugar to fruit. Now leave it to soak. Here's a rough time guide:

- Leave strong chilli, vanilla, cardamom or citrus for less than a day
- Hardy spices and strong-flavoured veg will need five to seven days
- Berries and strong fruit can take around three to four weeks to impart as much flavour as possible
- Milder ingredients such as apple or florals will take at least a month

When you're happy with the flavour, sieve to remove any solids, then pass through a very fine piece of muslin or a coffee filter to get rid of any sediment.

How to store: If your bottles or jars are well sealed, strained correctly and kept in a cool, dark place, your spirits can keep for up to a year.

Flavours for gin infusions can be drawn from seasonal or locally available fruits or herbs, or flavours that have wide-ranging appeal, such as oranges or other citrus fruit.

Cut up large fruit so the gin can be infused with the flavour more thoroughly. Leave it to steep for between a few days and a couple of months.

Transfer the finished gin to rinsed bottles. It is best to keep the gin in a cool, dark place, and then it will last for up to a year.

Sloe Gin

Sloe gin is the classic autumnal flavoured gin that most people have heard of, and it's the one that is created most often in kitchens up and down the land. The key to a good sloe gin is to prick the fruit all over before adding it to the alcohol. This can be time consuming but leads to a fuller fruit flavour. This gin should be left with the fruit infusing for up to three months to allow it to develop the deep, well rounded flavour that is so familiar to gin lovers. Many people like to add sugar as a sweetener at the beginning of the steeping process,

Sloe gin is often the first gin a keen gin drinker might make at home. It has now been produced professionally by a number of distilleries.

Sloes can be picked from British hedgerows in the autumn so are perfect to steep for a couple of months, in time to create a warming, spicy drink for the winter.

SLOE GIN RECIPE

500g sloes
250g sugar
70cl gin

- Wash the sloes and prick them all over to allow the juice to ooze into the gin
- Add them to a large clean jar or bottle along with the gin and the sugar
- Seal and leave in a dark place
- Agitate once a week until the sugar has dissolved
- Leave for at least three months before drinking to allow the flavours to develop

Sky Wave Gin collects rhubarb, when it is in season, from local Oxfordshire growers, for their raspberry and rhubarb gin. We prefer to use fresh fruit rather than flavourings.

which effectively turns the gin into a liqueur. The rule of thumb for sugar quantities is to use half the weight of the fruit for the sugar. So if you have 500g of sloes, add 250g of sugar. Sloe gin can happily sit for a number of months after it has been made, and some swear that this improves the flavour.

Once you've mastered the basic recipes, why not try our other imaginative infusions?

Creating Flavoured Gin Professionally

Sky Wave Gin introduced a raspberry and rhubarb gin to their range of gins early on. This was followed by a spiced apple gin liqueur. Both have been received very well by customers looking for something a little different.

So how do you create a professional flavoured gin?

Step One: Begin by creating your own gin, either via distillation or cold compounding.

Step Two: Consider the botanicals used in creating the gin, and add fruit, flavourings, herbs and spices that will complement them.

Step Three: Store in a food-grade container for one to three weeks, depending on the taste required.

Step Four: Strain or press the fruit. A range of options is available, from small hand presses to industrial hydraulic ones.

Sky Wave Gin creates fruit-flavoured gin by using their own distilled London Dry as a base for cold compounding.

The fruit and gin are stored in a food-grade container, where it macerates for between one and three weeks. It is placed in a cool, dark place during this time.

Having strained off the gin at the end of the maceration period, the fruit remains. The fruit juice is then extracted using a fruit press.

The fruit is contained in a mesh bag in the press. Weights are placed on top and manually screwed down, extracting the gin from the fruit at the bottom.

Step Five: Test the ABV of the flavoured gin, and correct it if necessary. Importantly, remember that with fruit content in the liquid, it becomes impossible to measure the ABV with an alcoholmeter as it will give an incorrect readings. So remember to record the absolute alcohol (AA) in the liquid before any process happens. Assuming that no liquid is lost during the process, then the alcohol will still be present at the end. Then calculate the ABV of the resultant liquid, based on the proportion of absolute alcohol present, and adjust the ABV according to the strength desired.

Step Six: Filter the gin through a filtration system to ensure it is free from any botanical residue. Sky Wave Gin use a professional bottling system that incorporates filters as part of the process.

Step Seven: Bottle and label.

Sky Wave Gin uses a large hydraulic fruit press, which can take industrial quantities of macerated fruit, again placed in a mesh bag, and extracts the liquid under pressure.

The fruit is pressed in a hydraulic fruit press and the apple-infused gin runs out at the bottom, to be collected for our spiced apple gin liqueur.

Raspberry and rhubarb gin is tested after the fruit is extracted, to ensure that the ABV is correct. Sky Wave Gin makes this fruit-flavoured gin a full-strength offering, at 42 per cent. Here, ethanol has been added to the liquid to bring it back up to strength.

To ensure there are no botanical residues or particles of fruit in flavoured gin it is important to filter the gin thoroughly. Sometimes the filtering process is incorporated in the bottling system.

Pink Gin

The new flavoured gins have enticed a much younger crowd to enjoy the tipple, lured by the sweet drinkability of the spirit and the desire to be showcasing the newest, hippest flavoured drink. Flavoured gin has found a new home on social media. The coolest, most original and most photogenic gins are rewarded with widespread praise on Instagram. But as it's all about the image, gin distillers are continually devising new iterations of their gin to appeal to the critical and fastidious new drinkers wanting the best images for their peers to approve. Some distilleries seem always to be chasing the next big trend.

Pink gin instigated the divergence from flavour to image, and has recently seen a resurgence in popularity, but it has evolved from its historical form to a different one, to match the shiny new world of gin drinkers. Traditionally a pink gin is a cocktail, which was very fashionable in the mid-nineteenth century. It consists of a gin with a dash of angostura bitters, which, being dark red, gives the whole drink an appealing pink hue.

But back to the modern-day pink gin. This catchall phrase now covers any gin that appears pink in colour, irrelevant of the flavour. In fact, many an artisan distiller

Pink gin has burst on to the market, offering an enticing image for cocktails and in many cases offering a sweeter gin, to attract the younger, non gin-drinking crowd.

THE ORIGINS OF PINK GIN

It is thought the origins of a pink gin lie with the British Royal Navy. Since the seventeenth century the navy was based at Plymouth, and sailors received Plymouth gin as part of their rations. This gin is sweeter than its counterpart London Dry Gin, and it was added to angostura bitters in the nineteenth century to help make the bitters more palatable, as they were used to treat sea sickness.

Pink gins have garnered a loyal following of drinkers, some who are attracted by the flavours, but others who are more swayed by the aesthetics of the gin.

has been dismayed when, after days, if not weeks or months of crafting a finely honed and delicately balanced gin infused with a variety of carefully chosen fruits, herbs and spices that combine to produce a fine gin with a rosy hue, he hears from one side of a busy bar on a Saturday night 'I'll have that pink gin there, please' – the perpetrator pointing at the aforementioned delicately crafted gin, oblivious to the flavours that lie within and set most definitely on its colour alone.

The pink gin market has seen a huge boom, and this has led to some wonderful creations with every fruit combination imaginable. Common ingredients include raspberries, rhubarb, strawberries and pink grapefruit. But then the boat is pushed out with pomegranate, pomelo, rose petals and pink peppercorns also being added. The final spirit can vary very much in its form and content. Sky Wave Gin produce a very dry raspberry and rhubarb pink gin, which, at 42 per cent, is a full-strength tipple. Local fruit growers know they can find a home for their surplus rhubarb with Sky Wave, in return for payment in gin: it's like a return to the old bartering system of payment – but way more fun! The 'pinkster gin' however, was one of the first, and arguably for a while, the best known gin, which traded purely by its name, on the colour of its offering. The fact that it contains red fruits was less important in the branding than the colour.

The addition of a 'pink gin' to an existing range has also helped some stalwarts of the gin industry to 'pep up' their brand. One of the grand-daddies of gin, Gordon's, which in the 1970s had a bottle in every drinks cabinet up and down the land, has quietly and with statesmanlike dignity retained its simple offering of the famous green bottle of London Dry Gin for many years. However, as the bar space around that classic green bottle exploded with increasingly exotic flavoured craft gins followed by the pink gin craze, Gordon's finally acquiesced and brought out a pink gin, its content defined by its colour, not its ingredients. It had an incredible effect on sales, which in turn helped make Gordon's the UK's second biggest spirit seller in 2018.

Sky Wave Gin crafts a full-strength raspberry and rhubarb gin with no added sugar and no added colouring. It was designed to be the antithesis of many overly sweet, pink gin liqueurs.

One of the oldest gins, Gordon's, eventually bowed to the popularist craze for pink gin, by bringing out its own. It unashamedly described its new tipple by its colour rather than its flavour – Gordon's pink gin.

In 2020, Bombay Sapphire, having stood firm against the pink deluge for a few years, finally threw in the towel with a flourish, announcing an 'Instagram ready' pack of miniature pink gin liqueurs. The company described the offer of four different flavours – rose, hibiscus, strawberry and raspberry – as 'trend based', and giving a 'rosy hue' to gin fans' tipples. It is interesting to note that the new floral gins in this particular pack were designed to be sweeter, possibly to attract those gin drinkers who are still developing their taste and are not so attracted to the dry, juniper flavour of a traditional London Dry. Also the way the gins looked was given more prominence in the description provided by Bombay Sapphire than the way the gins tasted. In its promotional literature, it describes the rose option as providing a 'subtle pink tone and floral notes', whilst the hibiscus liqueur offers a 'deeper, richer colour and aromatic taste'.

Novelty Gins

As the profile of gin drinkers gets younger, and the twenty-somethings are consumed by the never-ending quest to be seen looking fashionable and unique, distillers and drinks companies are producing ever more outlandish offerings.

The move away from at least the semblance of botanicals flavouring the evening gin and tonic culminated in the production of bubblegum gin. Its description, which is slightly at odds with an alcoholic drink, boasts that it 'takes you back to your childhood'. If you are wondering where it will stop, the answer is probably 'Who knows?'! Yes, there is also a chocolate gin – well, a cocoa gin – so the sky really is the limit.

Instagrammable Drinks

Younger gin drinkers discovering the fun and versatility of gin has led to its image changing. No longer just the preserve of smart, sophisticated advertising, gin has broken out, gone rogue, and found itself splashed across the pages of social media by its new Generation Z drinkers, keen to share their new discoveries. It helps that gins are served up in bars by master mixologists aiming to delight the eye, and consequently win followers for the social media-hungry generation consuming them. The epitome of this is the infamous Parma violet gin, which got rich on the back of Instagram. Its strong colour helped to make an impact on numerous Instagrammers' accounts – after all, who had seen a violet gin before? Once it is adorned with sweets and other garnishes it is extremely photogenic in a crowded market – it also stands out well on a supermarket shelf.

Unicorn Phenomenon

This mythical creature, formerly beloved of five-year-old girls, has been reimagined for the twenty-something gin-drinking generation. It all began with 'Unicorn Tears', a glittery gin flavoured with raspberries, which claims it is made with real unicorn tears. Leaving aside what caused the unicorn to cry, the drink is described as 'lip smackingly sweet', and therefore appealed to new gin drinkers who wanted great pictures for their social media account. Despite the sorrow experienced by the unicorn.

In other places, unicorns have fared a little better. Some have been locked in another form of pink gin, this time flavoured to taste of candy floss, but it would seem without the tears. The added twist to this gin is that it is marketed as a snow globe. The makers describe the gin liqueur as containing real 22-carat gold flakes and unicorn shimmer. Drinkers are encouraged to 'wow' their friends with this quirky gin. (It isn't clear how the unicorn felt.)

The pinnacle of this mythical beast-cum-novelty gin trend could be viewed as the pink-hued, unicorn-named gin, which glitters when poured, shaken or stirred, and tastes of marshmallow. The flavour is the result of toasted vanilla, and the glitter effect comes from a special type of edible protein. The gin purist will argue this drink has strayed as far from the origins of a London Dry as is possible. But still the creativity in gins continues, to attract more and more followers.

Colour-Changing Gins

In some quarters it would seem that a great-tasting, straightforward gin and tonic is no longer enough, and drinkers require theatrics from their aperitifs. Enter stage left the colour-changing gin. Drinkers

The new, younger generation of gin drinkers is on the lookout for the most Instagrammable cocktails with which to adorn their social-media pages.

Novelty gins have strayed far from traditional gin origins and branding. Unicorn Tears personifies a new type of gin, attracting those drinkers looking for something fun and unusual.

The mythical creature, the unicorn, has been adopted by some gins to attract more drinkers, mostly female and often twenty-something.

Forever searching for the next big thing to attract drinkers, gin companies have landed on colour-changing gin. The theatrics are much loved by a select range of drinkers.

start with a drink of one hue, and right before their eyes it changes into a different colour. It's all another perfect Instagrammable moment. So what's the secret? The magic happens when tonic is added. The acidic ingredient – the tonic – impacts the sensitive pH levels of the botanical blend, causing the colour to change right before your eyes. The trick is actually down to the distillery process, which is far simpler than you might think. The colour changing is due to the inclusion of flowers, which enable the colours to change from dark blue to pink when mixed. For example, one supermarket gin used the blue petals from the Asian butterfly flower in their gin. It meant the colour changed from pale sapphire to pink when the pH levels were altered with the addition of tonic or fruit.

Curiouser and Curiouser

Drinking gin in public has never been easier. Many bars have sprung up dedicated to just such a pastime over the past decade – many with one of two common themes: prohibition and curiosity. The former lends itself to bars with a 'speakeasy' feel, an American twist, designed to reflect the 1920s and 1930s, often located behind unassuming doors, sometimes with quirky access rituals such as locating and using a hidden telephone to add to the feeling of an illicit drinking den. The second theme, which pervades a number of gin establishments, is curiosity, usually reflecting the Victorians' keen interest in oddities, quirkiness and discovery. Bartenders dressed up in nineteenth-century costumes with an array of moustaches, shake and pour cocktails with bursts of excitement mixed with refined service. The decoration of these places often reflects a gentleman's library with his treasured artefacts, gathered from around the world, on display.

It is this fad for curious Victorian drinking clubs that has spawned some new flavours to match. Most recently Hendricks gin has brought out its 'Lunar' gin, described as having been conceived 'beneath the celestial light of the moon, and yielding an alluring complexity and a delightful warmth'. It follows hot on the heels of its 'Midsummer Solstice Gin' in 2019. As some flavours become brasher and more obvious, it is clear that some gins wish to push their offerings into creative new taste experiences.

Where Now for Flavoured Gins?

There has been a huge turnaround in the demand for flavoured alcoholic drinks in the beverage market. In the mid-1990s you couldn't move for flavoured vodkas, and drinkers only had the choice of about four gins. Now it is the reverse. A whole section of drinkers, mostly new to gin, expect their gin to be flavoured with something other than juniper, and preferably to be pink or purple. Mythical creatures of varying emotions are optional but encouraged.

In our experience at Sky Wave Gin we have found a huge divide in the drinking population of Great Britain. One swathe of the population, usually under forty, are on the lookout for a flavoured gin – the more exotic or unusual the better. If you mention the words 'London Dry' they look blank, and don't understand what it means. Or at worst proffer those soul-destroying words to an artisan gin distiller: 'Oh, you mean the ordinary one?' However, there is also a good section of keen purists who love their London Dry and other 'ordinary' gins, and take immense pleasure from detecting and discussing the delicate balance of botanicals that go into their classic 'G&T'.

Whatever excites drinkers is good for the industry, so whether it's stepping into the equivalent of a sweet shop and choosing by colour or weird flavour, as compared to knowing your junipers and opting for a classic juniper-led gin, it's all good for the ever-growing sector and its dedicated distillers.

CHAPTER 8

WHEN THINGS GO WRONG

When you begin distilling gin, it's a fact of life that things will not always go according to plan. It is inevitable. There is an old saying that if brewing beer is biology, then distilling gin is chemistry – and complex chemistry at that. There are so many elements to consider in the process. There is the type of neutral grain spirit you choose to use, the botanicals you select, the ratio of those botanicals, maintaining the correct temperature in your still, the interactions your botanicals have with each other, the method and equipment you choose to use: all of these will have an effect on the outcome of your gin. In this chapter we consider some of the things that may go wrong when you create your gin. We have experienced most of them, and have researched and worked through the solutions with much patience and with many tweaks to our recipes and production methods.

TASTE PROBLEMS

There could be a number of reasons why your gin doesn't taste as you had hoped. We highlight a few here, and suggest some remedies.

Cutting the Tails

One of the reasons a gin may not taste as good as you'd hoped, or is inconsistent from batch to batch, could be down to when the tails were cut. This part of the distillation process, at the end of the still run, can produce bitter-tasting oils. This spirit is usually collected separately after the hearts and reintroduced to the still for the next batch, where the bitterness is stripped away. If cut properly, then, this bitterness shouldn't get into your bottled product.

There is a real art to knowing when to cut the heads and the tails. During the distillation process, the flavour of different botanicals comes through at different times in the run. A distiller will need to judge each stage of the distillation to know when to make the cuts. As we have discussed, larger distilleries may make them on alcohol content (ABV) alone, whereas craft distillers may pride themselves on making the cut by taste. If they get it wrong and cut too late, then bitterness will creep into the finished gin.

Learning when to cut by taste is a skill gained only by experience. Unfortunately, if you have cut too late, there is little you can do to recover the batch itself. You might consider reusing the batch in the wash for your next still run, but remember (assuming you use the normal quantities of botanicals in this subsequent run) you will have approaching double the essential oils in the finished distillate, and must cut it accordingly, as if you had used the concentrate method of production. This will not be an exact science, and it is unlikely that your finished gin will be exactly the same as all your other unspoilt batches.

Botanicals

The first taste problem caused by your botanicals might simply be that the recipe just doesn't work, and you may need to go back to the design of the flavour profile. Consider which botanicals you have chosen, and also their proportions. Remember, for example, that when distilled in gin, botanicals don't always produce the flavour or aroma you might expect from their normal state. Alternatively, perhaps it could be the combination of the botanicals you have used – some combinations just don't work together.

If you're sure that you have replicated your recipe and processes exactly, yet a later batch doesn't taste like an earlier batch, perhaps your botanicals are different or from a different source. For example, did you realize there are more than fifty species of juniper, with *Juniperus communis*, common juniper, being the variety most usually used in gin?

Furthermore the flavour of botanicals can vary quite widely between different countries of origin, so try to stay consistent in your supply. Remember also that poor storage can affect botanicals quite markedly: conditions that are too damp or too warm can cause even dried botanicals to deteriorate.

If you can't taste a signature botanical in your gin as expected, then consider whether you have used enough of it, or if it isn't being swamped by more dominant botanicals. Again, you may have to revisit the design of your flavour profile.

Has My Gin Gone Off?

Poor taste cannot come from gin 'going off', because the good news is that gin doesn't – that is, if it's a proper gin, at 37.5 per cent ABV or more. (Liqueurs, however, are a different story.) The alcohol content ensures that, whilst bacteria could exist, they can't thrive. Even fruit gins won't go mouldy! It can settle, yes, and sediment can form. It can change colour in sunlight (especially if very rich in botanicals or real fruit), and a host of other things could happen to its appearance – but it can't go off. So that, at least, is not a factor in any taste problem.

Are *You* The Problem?

The single greatest reason why your gin may taste different from one day to the next is *you*! Humans do not taste consistently. Our sense of taste can vary from one day to the next, or even from hour to hour: what you've eaten, how hydrated you are, whether your body is fighting an illness – all of these can affect your sense of taste. So if what tasted good yesterday tastes a bit 'off' today, try it again tomorrow before making a decision.

WHAT'S THAT IN MY GIN?

Cloudiness

A gin going slightly cloudy when you add your mixer is perfectly normal – it's called louching – and some distilleries, such as The Cotswold Distillery or Garden Swift from the Capreolus Distillery, make a feature of it. It is caused by the essential oils dropping out of suspension in the alcohol when the mixer is added, and is a mark of a gin full of flavour, one full of the essential oils from the botanicals. The technical explanation involves the fact that these oils are medium-long chain ethyl esters, or fatty acids – but we don't need to go into that level of detail here.

However, you may find that your gin louches in your production process when you cut the distillate to your serving strength, and this is less desirable. Customers will probably not buy a gin that's cloudy in the bottle, no matter how much you try to convince them that it's the flavour. Moreover, you may find that over time the louche dissipates slightly but a sediment forms on the bottom of the bottle – again probably undesirable.

Gin will louche at the cutting stage simply because the concentration of essential oils is too great for the amount of alcohol in solution. It is the alcohol that holds the oils in solution, and when water is added the alcohol is able to hold less of them, and so they fall out. Oil in water is cloudy, and that's what you see.

There are three options to solve this particular problem. You have effectively created a concentrate, so you can either: a) use smaller quantities of botanicals in your recipe; or b) add more neutral spirit after distillation (as per the concentrate method of production); or c) use a higher ABV in your still. This last ensures that there is more alcohol available in the distillate to hold the oils, and is effectively the complement of the first.

Sediment

There are three reasons why sediment could be present in your gin: problems during distillation; too great a quantity of botanicals for the alcohol; or poor filtration.

Here the gin has louched (gone extremely cloudy) when cut with water to bottling strength. This is caused by the oils dropping out of suspension as the new water bonds with the ethanol. It is caused by the gin being too concentrated in botanicals.

Problems During Distillation

Your distillate should be crystal clear. If the still is running properly, only the purest spirit should be being produced. If your distillate is coloured or contains sediment, something has gone wrong. First, you may not have cleaned your still thoroughly from the previous run. You may have collected particles of botanicals in the column, lyne arm or condenser, and these have been flushed through at the start of the run. One of the reasons to collect heads is partly to ensure that this flushing process has been done.

Second, your still may have 'boiled over'. This is much easier to do with small stills because the diameter of the surface area of the wash tends to be similar to the diameter of the column – when it happens, it goes straight up the column. It is also more likely in very full stills where the surface of the wash is almost up to the column – for this reason, never fill a still to the brim.

It can happen for a number of reasons, including applying too much heat too quickly to the kettle, forgetting to cool the condenser with cold water, or foaming of your wash. The first two of these are relatively easily fixed.

Heat the still gently. Don't rush to achieve the flow of distillate, and once at temperature, maintain it at around 80°C. Think of the process as rather like boiling a pan of rice: you want it to simmer steadily, but not boil over.

Also, ensure that the coolant water for the condenser is flowing well before distillate vapours are present

Distillate will stop being clear due to the presence of botanicals passing over into the condenser and on into the distillate. Something has gone wrong with the distillation process and it should be stopped and corrected immediately.

in the condenser. If the condenser is not cooling the vapours, then the build-up of pressure can result in the kettle boiling over. This is because the vapours are at a higher pressure than the liquid in the wash, expanding as they turn to vapour. They escape ultimately through the condenser, and are normally returned to a lower pressure liquid (the distillate) by being cooled in the condenser, thus reducing the pressure across the system.

However, in the event that they are *not* condensed back to a liquid, because the condenser tube is normally much narrower than the column, the pressure increases. If this is happening, steam will be seen emerging from the distillate outflow, often at some force, a sure sign that the coolant water is not flowing, or is flowing too slowly to extract the heat from the distillate and cause it to condense, or that the heat source to the kettle is too high. As the still boils over, it forces the wash up through the column, lyne arm and condenser, and contaminates the distillate with discoloured wash and sediment. This could happen very obviously, or really quite subtly, and is only noticed by discoloration of the distillate.

To prevent this, again only heat the still gently, and maintain the temperature at around 80°C; also, ensure the coolant water for the condenser is flowing well before the distillate flows, and is of sufficient flow to cool and condense the distillate. As a rule of thumb, if you have an open cup style of condenser, ensure that the water always feels cool to a dipped finger. If you have a closed Liebig-style condenser, it should be cool to the touch along its length.

Foaming of your wash is harder to manage, and again requires careful temperature control. Foaming happens because of certain physical properties of botanicals, normally powders. At certain concentrations of alcohol, water and the botanical or botanicals in question, the wash starts to foam around these powders. Bubbles form, which can become large and ultimately rise up the column. This creates a pressure build-up as the foam briefly seals the column, and the wash boils over and up the column, rushing over into the distillate. Again you will see discoloration and particles in the distillate.

Commercial distillers employ agitators in their stills, which can, amongst other things, help to disrupt foaming; but this is unlikely to be available to the craft distiller. For us, the solution is very careful temperature control. If your still has a sight glass, watch for the foam forming. If not, listen carefully to the still to hear a change in sound as the bubbles form and burst. This is the critical time to react: at this point, back off the heat source and let the bubbles settle, then gently reapply the heat until the distillate flows gently again. If the wash foams again, keep repeating the process of reducing the heat until the foaming no longer happens (because you have gone past the point of critical concentrations) and the still run can continue as normal. It is, of course, possible to adjust your recipe to avoid the problem botanicals or specific concentrations of them, but this may not be desirable. Thankfully, foaming like this is relatively rare.

Too Great a Quantity of Botanicals

If the sediment is only evident after a period of time sitting on the shelf, and if your gin louches quite heavily when mixed with water or a mixer, then the sediment is probably from having too high a quantity of botanicals: you have essentially produced a concentrate. The oils fall out of suspension in the bottle and settle on the bottom, often as a darker, brownish-looking stain. Shaking the bottle may cause them to be re-dissolved, but the discoloration of the gin may remain.

Alternatively, small white particles may form in your gin. These could be so pronounced that it can look almost like a snow globe. This is again due to an excess of botanical oils, and is called flocculation. The essential oils from the botanicals have been mentioned numerous times, but the flavours also come from botanical waxes. These waxes (perfectly harmless, edible, and in fact, part of where the flavour comes from) can coalesce into tiny particles, which gather others and eventually become large enough to be visible. This often happens over many months, and so is extremely difficult to detect at the point of production. They won't affect the flavour and are harmless to drink. They can be caused not only by over-rich quantities of botanicals, but also by too harsh or rushed distillation. As always, the key is to distil slowly, gently, and at the correct temperatures.

Contrary to popular belief, by the way, these particles are not bacteria, nor are they from the use of cork stoppers.

The formation of particles can be reduced or eliminated by cold filtration, whereby the gin is chilled in a freezer and then filtered. The chilling

White particles in bottles of gin like this are caused by flocculation, where the oils and waxes from the botanicals clump together over time. Whilst this is perfectly harmless and the gin is entirely drinkable, it is nonetheless unattractive in a commercial gin. It is generally caused by the botanicals being too concentrated.

causes this process to accelerate and clump the waxes together, thus allowing them to be filtered more easily. Ultimately, however, the best and purest approach to solving this problem is skilful distillation using appropriate quantities of botanicals.

Poor Filtration

All gins should be filtered by food-grade filters at the point of bottling to ensure they are fit for human consumption. Depending on the method of production (distillation, cold compounding, fruit maceration after distillation), the gin may have been filtered a number of times prior to that. If the filtration processes are lacking, then sediment may be able to pass through. The key to fixing this issue is to use filters of an appropriate grade – for a dry gin, at the bottling stage use professional filters of at least 0.5 microns.

Poor filtration can cause particles to be visible in the gin and sediment to form on the bottom of the bottle. Whilst some sediment is acceptable in fruit gins, it is generally undesirable in dry gins.

DISCOLORATION

We have already discussed cloudiness and sediment, but gin can also change colour over time. Crystal-clear dry gin can start to yellow, and fruit gins can fade in colour or turn brown.

Clear gin will discolour for two reasons, often both simultaneously. As described above, the over-presence of botanical oils, too much to be held permanently in solution by the alcohol, may cause oils to drop out. These will normally drop to the bottom, but could stay in suspension. Depending on the makeup of these oils, the second process may then happen: these oils may react to light and could darken or yellow over time, causing the gin to become less than crystal clear. There is a reason why a lot of gin is not served in clear bottles! To prevent this, refine the recipe and store bottles in a cool, dark place away from heat and direct sunlight.

For fruit gins, it is a fact that the juice of fruit, especially red fruit, darkens and turns brown in light. Commercial producers get round this by using extracted flavourings and essences rather than actual fruit, but craft producers often want the provenance of using fresh fruit with no additives. The only way to prevent this discoloration is, again, to ensure that bottles are stored in a cool, dark place away from heat and direct sunlight.

MAINTAINING ABV

This section isn't strictly about something going wrong, but it does highlight a potential pitfall and explains how to avoid it.

Ensuring that the gin is at the ABV claimed is critical for when it is sold commercially. Trading standards will take a dim view of your claiming an ABV that is different from their findings, especially if it is lower than advertised. Yet ensuring that the ABV is correct can seem to be a challenge, especially for fruit and compounded gins.

The issue is that, when you add fruit, fruit juices or other ingredients to your gin that change the overall volume, this will change the ABV. Moreover, once you have fruit content in the liquid, it becomes impossible to measure the ABV with an alcoholmeter – they do not work with any liquid that isn't pure water and ethanol, and give incorrect readings.

The secret is to remember what ABV stands for – alcohol by volume. Start by ensuring that the absolute alcohol (AA) in the liquid is recorded before any process, whether it's compounding or adding fruit juice. Assuming that no liquid is lost during the process, then the alcohol will still be present at the end. It is then possible to calculate the ABV of the resultant liquid based on the proportion of absolute alcohol present, and advertise or adjust the ABV accordingly. For example, in 1,000ml of gin at 42 per cent ABV, the AA is 420ml. If 100ml of fruit juice is then added, the ABV goes down to 38.18 per cent. The result should either be advertised as such, or neutral spirit added to bring it back up to 42 per cent.

HM Revenue
& Customs

Excise Processing Teams
HM Revenue and Customs
BX9 1GL

Phone 0300 200 3700

Web www.gov.uk

Date 28 August 20XX
Our Ref XXXXX

Licence L110 to carry on an excise trade

Licence number:	XXX/C/XXX/XX
This licence allows you to carry on the excise trade:	Compounder of Spirits
Excise ID:	N/A
From:	27/08/XX

The licensed premises:
XXXXXXX

XXXXX XXXXX
Officer of HM Revenue and Customs

CHAPTER 9

LICENCE TO DISTIL

In most countries and territories, to produce any form of gin you must be licensed. In fact, in the UK you will need as many as six different licences, depending on how you make your gin and what you want to do with it after you've produced it – for example, if you want to sell it. You also need to comply with various other standards and regulations, and your operation may be subject to inspection at any time by the various authorities.

This chapter focuses on regulations within the UK, but most other countries adopt similar approaches, and you are strongly encouraged to research your local laws and regulations before proceeding to distil gin and offer it for sale. Please note that nothing in this chapter should be considered legally binding or formal legal advice, nor does it claim to be complete in all respects regarding complying with the law in your country, including the UK. You remain responsible for all your own licensing, and for ensuring that you meet appropriate national and local standards and regulations.

For producers of any scale, there are numerous licences to obtain in order to launch as a business, however small. In the UK the bureaucracy is detailed and lengthy, and many a bar or distillery has had to delay its opening, as obtaining all the necessary licences doesn't always happen quickly; in fact it often happens painfully slowly as there are other factors involved, and all have to come together at the right time.

There are organizations that offer to obtain all your necessary licences for you, for a fee. You might consider using such services, and they will help prevent costly mistakes being made. Remember, however, that some licences, especially from HMRC in the UK, are free. You are therefore paying mostly only for expertise in navigating the bureaucracy.

Licences in the UK fall into two main categories: licences from HMRC to protect the Revenue; and licences from the local authority to ensure proper control of people and premises selling alcohol, and food standards. We discuss each category in turn. But before we do, let's have a quick look at the history of licensing of gin producers, and the collection of duty on alcohol, in the UK.

THE HISTORY OF LICENSING AND DUTY FOR ALCOHOL

Alcohol has been taxed throughout the ages by different governments. Often it was a means to an end, a way to raise money for the government from a product that was highly desirable. However, the higher the taxes imposed on alcohol, the greater the rate of smuggling. Gin was in fact at the very heart of one of the original reasons for imposing duty on alcohol. At the end of the seventeenth century cheap gin was being drunk in vast quantities across Britain. This was partly because new laws introduced by William III encouraged gin distillation, having banned the importation of French brandy due to ongoing conflicts with France. Another reason that gin was being drunk so widely and by so many was because it became part of workers' wages. Soon more people in Britain, and especially London, were drinking more gin than beer.

However, the widespread consumption of gin caused serious health and social problems, as the poor working class that had flocked to the capital to find work in the newly emerging factories enjoyed the escape the alcohol provided from their new lives. These new lives were often not as these people had hoped, due to poor living and working conditions, and it is thought that gin was one of the main causes behind the death rate in the capital overtaking the birth rate at this time. So in the first half of the eighteenth century gin sellers were required to be licensed, and the duty on gin was raised from 2d per gallon to 2s per gallon. By 1736 the cost of a licence was raised to £50 and duty to £1, making gin prohibitively expensive.

For the next fifteen years gin continued to be drunk in vast quantities, almost always from unlicensed outlets, and often dangerously made, with hazardous cheap additions to bulk out the spirit. A new system of regulation was introduced in 1751 along with a change in the economic environment, which led to a more stable period.

Leaping forwards to 1992, and the start of the EU single market is the direct reason why duty stamps were introduced on alcohol products. For the first time the British were able to travel more freely to other European countries, where alcohol was much cheaper, due to lower duties. This led to a huge increase in what was effectively small-scale smuggling by British citizens, who brought back huge quantities of alcohol, which they were able to do under the legal loophole of claiming it was 'for personal use'. But then the alcohol would be sold on illegally in Britain without the duty being paid. By 2003 the government had announced plans whereby bottles were required to display a stamp confirming that the UK duty had been paid. Measures to enforce this were included in the 2004 Finance Bill.

HMRC LICENSING

The first port of call for anyone wanting to research licences should be HMRC's 'Excise Notice 39: spirits production in the UK'. According to this – and strictly speaking, even if you are creating sloe gin in a jar in the kitchen for your friends and family to enjoy – you will need a licence because you are taking one form of alcohol (gin) and turning it into another, different alcoholic drink. According to the words of HMRC, you are 'combining or mixing plain spirits or previously compounded spirits with any other substance, except water, so as to distinctly alter the character or flavour of the plain spirits or compounded spirits, producing a new compounded spirit.' This is cold compounding, and requires an HMRC compounder's licence.

There are different licensing requirements depending on whether you want to conduct a (relatively) simple process such as re-distilling neutral spirit, known as rectifying, or if you are planning on making your own base spirit. Distilling from scratch involves obtaining a distiller's licence, which is rarely granted to craft premises. It would also mean having a fully bonded storage facility approved as an excise warehouse as part of the distillery set-up. As creating your own base spirit is a larger, more costly and more complex route to making gin, this chapter will focus on the more common route taken by craft gin distillers: rectification and compounding of neutral spirit sourced elsewhere.

Rectifier's Licence

A rectifier's licence allows a distiller to re-distil spirits. This definition can be quite confusing – as *distilling* spirits is exactly what you want to do – so what's this re-distilling all about? Remember that to distil gin, a neutral base spirit is used, and that has already been distilled. So as far as HMRC is concerned, you are re-distilling this neutral spirit when you distil gin. To put it simply, it's all about protecting the revenue. There is a very high rate of excise duty to be paid on alcohol, and HMRC needs to ensure that duty is paid on all spirits produced for human consumption at every appropriate stage of the process of production. This, and ensuring that only 'fit and proper persons' are involved, is what licensing is all about. So in short, and to be clear, to *distil* gin using heat and a still, and using neutral spirit and botanicals, you will need a rectifier's licence.

To obtain a rectifier's licence it is necessary to apply to HMRC, and this can be done online. A rectifier's licence can be applied for individually (as a sole trader) or as another legal entity, such as a partnership or limited company. It should be noted that a rectifier's licence applies to all of the following, in combination: the legal entity; the specific activity; a specified location; and a specified piece of equipment. Therefore if any of those elements changes, the licence ceases to be valid and must be applied for anew. For example, if the distillery moves premises, or upgrades the still, then a new licence should be applied for. A licence application must be accompanied by a plan of the building in which the operation will take place, and a description of the plant to be used; this is known as 'making entry'.

It is worth noting that it can take up to six weeks from application to obtaining your licence – if indeed it is approved. The good news is that the licence is free.

Compounder's Licence

As we have illustrated, to produce a flavoured gin at home by steeping some fruit in gin and selling it, even just at local markets, requires a compounder's licence. This is required by HMRC if you substantially change the character or flavour with another substance, other than water – for example fruit – and don't use a still in the process. You must also complete an excise 'entry' and have it approved by HMRC before you can start compounding. As for the compounder's licence, it is necessary to apply to HMRC, and this can be done online. Again, it can take up to six weeks from application to obtaining your licence, and it is free.

Bonding

Bonding is the process whereby HMRC accepts that alcohol on which duty is due to be paid can be held 'in bond', and that duty will be paid at the appropriate point in the future. This is usually at the point of wholesale or retail sale. Bonded status is awarded by HMRC to specific legal entities, usually limited companies, for specific premises. The certifying and inspection regimes are strict – again, to protect the revenue. Premises need to be highly secure, and records need to be kept of every drop of alcohol at every stage of the production process. For these reasons it is extremely unlikely that bonded status would be awarded by HMRC to anything but purpose-built or heavily adapted premises.

To avoid these requirements, almost all craft distillers buy in their neutral spirit duty paid. This means that the duty is already paid at the point of purchase and the Revenue is satisfied. It does make the neutral spirit very expensive, however, as 84 per cent of the cost is duty; but the benefits are clear. The downside of the approach is that it makes the process financially inefficient. As it is impossible to extract and use 100 per cent of the alcohol, there is always going to be some waste – and the duty cannot be recovered on that waste. This is one reason why commercially produced gin will always be cheaper than craft gin.

Alcohol Wholesalers Registration Scheme

If you wish to sell your craft gin anywhere else but directly to your end consumers – that is, to shops, pubs, bars and restaurants – then you will need to be registered with the Alcohol Wholesalers Registration Scheme (AWRS). The scheme was introduced by HMRC in 2015 to tackle alcohol fraud, and failure to register and comply with its legal regulations.

The key aspect here is that you cannot trade in alcohol wholesaling until you get approval. Time plays another important role: you must apply to HMRC giving at least forty-five days' notice. When you apply for approval you will need to pass what it describes as a 'fit and proper' test. You cannot sell your gin to wholesalers until you get approval.

The Fit and Proper Test

HMRC will only issue approval to people they believe have shown themselves to be fit and proper to carry out the business specified. HMRC will want to reassure itself that the business is genuine, and that all those involved in it are law abiding and don't pose any risk in terms of fraud. HMRC will conduct a telephone interview with the individual applying to register with the scheme. The interview aims to ensure that you understand your duties with regard to complying with the regulations, including due diligence checks on your suppliers, with the necessary record keeping, and that you are 'fit and proper'. You cannot have a criminal record, or have any outstanding tax affairs, or be in any other way unsuitable to HMRC.

You must also be able to provide details of your suppliers, customers, business plans, accounting and stock control systems, premises, and financial viability. There can be a somewhat 'chicken and egg' situation here, in that you cannot sell to shops and pubs without registration with the scheme, and yet HMRC requires details of your customers. This can be difficult for a small craft distillery just starting out, as no one will want to buy your gin until you're licensed. A way around it is to obtain 'letters of intent' from three friendly outlets (pubs and shops) who are willing to state that they intend to buy from you as soon as you are licensed.

Once the decision has been made, you will be sent a letter that includes details of your registered number: this consists of four letters and eleven numbers – for example, XXAW00000123456. You will need to include this AWRS number on your invoices, and you may also be asked to show it to new wholesale customers if they request it.

In return, you should ask for, and keep a record of, all your suppliers of alcohol – and this includes not only when you start to buy in your neutral spirit, but also your suppliers of vodka if that is how you intend to start out.

Duty Stamps

Excise stamps are mostly found on tobacco and alcohol products. They show that the required excise, or duty, has been paid by the manufacturer to the relevant authority. In the UK, duty stamps are again issued by HMRC. The stamps are very detailed in their design, and in the same way as banknotes, are created to avoid counterfeiting. Displaying a duty stamp on a product helps to guarantee that it is genuine, as only a certified producer may legally display the stamps. Naturally, HMRC only approves duty

Gin with an alcohol by volume of more than 30 per cent in bottles of 350ml or more will legally require a duty stamp on every bottle.

stamps for those producers whom it has been proved are paying the appropriate duty.

If your gin has an alcohol by volume of more than 30 per cent (which it should do, as the minimum ABV for a gin, to be able to call itself a gin, is 37.5 per cent) in bottles of 350ml or more, then you will need to make sure they have a duty stamp on every bottle. These stickers are required by law if your product is intended for consumption in Britain. The labels are free to obtain from HMRC, or they can be incorporated into your label design. You will need to supply information such as your VAT registration number if you have one, your Excise ID number, if you have one, and indicate how many free-standing stamps you expect to order in the next twelve months. When HMRC have received your application, they will issue you with a registration number and then you will be able to request your stamps. Again, planning ahead and leaving enough time helps to avoid delays in bringing your gin to market.

Record Keeping

In the UK and most other territories, you are required to keep thorough records of all alcohol transactions, including all stock received, all supplier due diligence checks, product produced, product sold, and all uses of free-standing duty stamps. These records should be available for inspection at any time. Whilst the regulations do not specify exactly how these records should be kept, they are quite complex, and you are advised to research them thoroughly to avoid falling foul of the law. Again, search the internet for HMRC's 'Excise Notice 39: spirits production in the UK' as the first place to seek guidance.

LOCAL AUTHORITY LICENCES

Personal Licence

To go to the next step, beyond the mere *production* of gin, requires yet more licences. If you want to sell or supply your gin in England and Wales then you must have a licence or other authorization from a licensing authority – usually a local council. The different licences are:

- a **personal licence** for anyone who intends to sell alcohol or authorize the sale of alcohol
- a **premises licence** for any business that permanently sells alcohol

The HMRC website is the first point of call for applying for a licence – you will need to complete an application form and send it to your local council, along with the fee. You may also need to send copies of your form (depending on the type of application you are making) to the police and other authorities, listed below under 'Applying for a Premises Licence'.

Taking a closer look at the personal licence, it is designed to ensure that anybody running or managing a business that sells or supplies alcohol will do it in a business-like and responsible way. When you are in receipt of your personal licence, you are the designated premises supervisor for any business that sells or supplies alcohol.

Who Can Apply?

If you are applying for a personal licence, you must be over eighteen years old, and must ensure you have got the right accredited qualification beforehand. This qualification aims to make sure that licence holders are aware of many aspects around selling alcohol, including the licensing law and wider social responsibilities. Personal licence qualification providers are accredited by the Home Secretary, and you can find a range of them online.

When you apply for your personal licence your local council will want to know if you have any relevant criminal convictions. If you do, and depending what these are, it may mean that the authority is unable to grant you a licence. You will also need to provide a criminal conviction disclosure form. It is important to time the application for this carefully, as the form must be dated within one month of your application being submitted. When you are applying for your personal licence, do it to the council in whose district you *live*, which is not necessarily the same council as where the distillery or distillery shop is located. This may seem counter-intuitive, but HMRC describe it as akin to holding a driving licence but being able to drive any car – your personal licence allows you to be the designated supervisor of *any* (and multiple) licensed premises. Your application will also need to include two passport photos and show that you have the right to work in the UK.

Licensing Qualification

To gain the personal licence holder's qualification, you are required to take, and pass, a course. Courses are available from a range of accredited providers, a list of which can be found via the HMRC website. The course provides the necessary learning to complete the Level 2 award for personal licence holders. It covers a range of topics, including a full overview of alcohol licensing; applying for an alcohol licence; alcohol and its effects; personal licence holder responsibilities, protecting vulnerable people from alcohol; working in partnership; licensing for temporary events; and understanding prohibitions and exemptions.

The course covers a lot of useful information, which you will need to know if you are looking to sell your gin. Courses may be provided by private course providers, but the other, more economical alternative is to apply through your local authority. The course work is usually supplied online, and you should set aside four to six hours for learning and revision.

The course requires learners to sit a one-hour exam. This is usually organized by the licensing department in your local authority, and will be held in a council building. Prices vary, depending on whether the qualification is taken privately or through the local authority.

Once the course exam has been successfully completed, applicants can apply for a personal licence from their local authority. This comes as two parts: a paper copy and a card copy.

Premises Licence

A premises licence allows the use of any premises for licensable activities, as defined in Section 1 of the Licensing Act 2003. The premises do not have to be a physical building, which is useful if you want to sell at markets or festivals. Here is a helpful list of venues for which a premises licence can be granted:

- Movable structures such as a beer tents and burger vans
- Open spaces such as fields for festivals
- Vessels such as river and canal boats

Once you have been granted a premises licence, it will be valid until:

- the licence is revoked
- the premises licence holder becomes incapacitated or goes bankrupt
- the licence is formally surrendered to the licensing authority

Applying for a Premises Licence

Like the personal licence, you must be eighteen years or older to apply for a premises licence. You would apply to the local authority in the area where the venue will operate. You will be asked to complete an application form, to include a floorplan of the premises, and to send the application fee. It is worth spending a moment on the floorplan element of the application. The form will ask you to identify the parts of the building where you will be selling your gin. When Sky Wave Gin applied, we were advised that as we were planning to sell online from our home, which is also where the distillery is based, we might, realistically, make that transaction via our laptop in any room on the ground floor. So we needed to include a floor plan of the entire ground floor of the house, not just the distillery itself.

When you apply for an application for a premises licence the application will ask you to show how you will promote the four 'licensing objectives'. You will have learned about these through the personal licence course. It will also ask you to carry out the appropriate risk assessments to make sure that they comply with any specific requirements on which you may have been advised by the police or fire services.

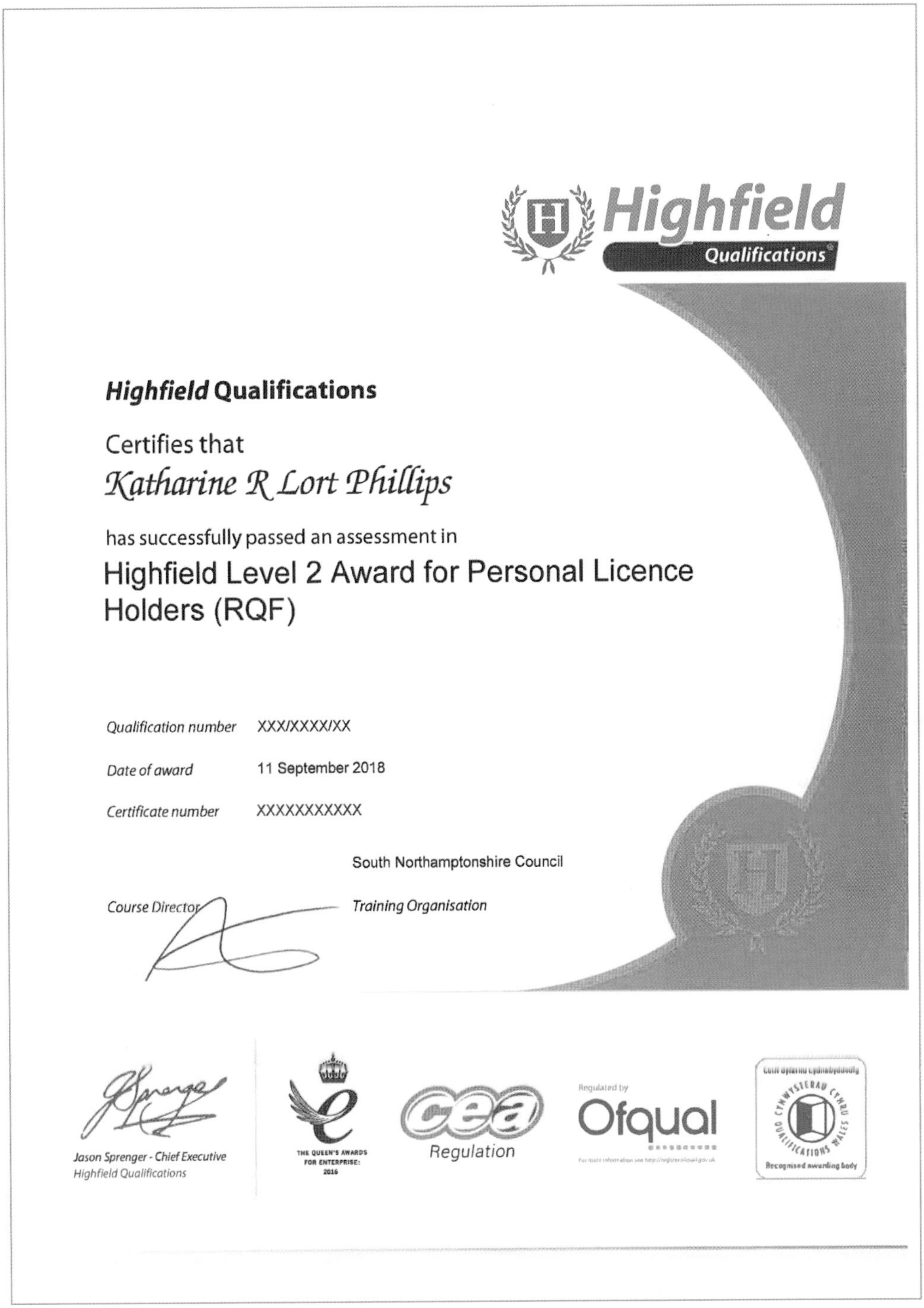

Highfield Qualifications

Highfield Qualifications

Certifies that

Katharine R Lort Phillips

has successfully passed an assessment in

Highfield Level 2 Award for Personal Licence Holders (RQF)

Qualification number XXX/XXXX/XX

Date of award 11 September 2018

Certificate number XXXXXXXXXXX

Course Director

South Northamptonshire Council

Training Organisation

Jason Sprenger - Chief Executive
Highfield Qualifications

THE QUEEN'S AWARDS FOR ENTERPRISE: 2016

cea Regulation

Regulated by Ofqual

Recognised awarding body

Many licences are required before gin production can commence. The personal licence is the next step and enables the gin producer to sell their products. It entails a written exam.

Your application will go back to the local authority and then be circulated to the official bodies listed below for consideration:

- Police licensing officer
- Fire officer
- Health and safety officer
- Environmental health officer
- Planning officer
- Child protection officer
- Trading standards (also known as Weights and Measures)
- Primary care trust or local health board

It is worth bearing in mind that as a result, you may get an unannounced call from any of the above authorities, who will wish to talk to you further about any aspect of your application. When Sky Wave Gin made its application, we had unannounced phone calls from the fire service, the police and the local council planning department.

We also had an unannounced visit from an environmental health officer wanting to inspect our premises and see our hazard analysis and critical control point (HACCP). We are pleased to say we were awarded a top score of 5 for food hygiene. These scores are made public by the local authority, and some local newspapers publish them weekly, for all to see, so it is worth making sure you have done your research, have a good HACCP plan in place, and are always maintaining the appropriate standards.

Finally, a notice summarizing the premises licence application must be advertised in the local paper and at the premises themselves. This notice should include

Any premises where gin is made will be under scrutiny and could receive a visit from the environmental health officer; food hygiene ratings are subsequently awarded. Sky Wave Gin received the top score of 5.

Notice of Application under Section 17 of the Licensing Act 2003
Katharine Rachel Lort-Phillips of Cheveley, Bucknell, Oxon OX27 7LU Propose to Licence these Premises to sale of alcohol. Representations can be made in writing by 14.09.18 to The Licensing Authority, Cherwell District Council Bodicote House, Bodicote, Banbury, Ox15 4AA. Tel: 01295 753744, E-Mail: licensing@cherwell-dc.gov.uk Web: www.cherwell.gov.uk
Full details of the application can be inspected by appointment at the address above. It is an offence knowingly or recklessly to make a false statement in connection with an application and the maximum fine for which a person is liable on summary conviction of the offence is not exceeding £5,0000

Legally a gin company must publicise its application for a premises licence – one of the many licences needed to produce and sell gin – by taking out a notice in the local newspaper.

details of the premises, the licensable activities applied for, the intended opening hours, where the application can be viewed, and contact details of the licensing authority. Following the notice period, which is often around twenty-eight days, the licensing authority will consider the application.

When the premises licence does arrive, you will need to display it where it can be easily seen, and there are some nasty fines if you do not. The police and the council can ask to inspect the details of your licence at any time.

TRADING STANDARDS AND OTHER COMPLIANCE

As well as meeting all the licensing regulations, you must be compliant with a raft of trading standards and other rules. For example, you must ensure that the ABV of your product is precisely as advertised on your labels and elsewhere. You must ensure that you meet food hygiene standards throughout, including in the bottling and storage parts of your operation. You must meet labelling requirements, and you may wish to adhere to the Portman Group code of conduct for alcohol producers.

Labelling Requirements

The labelling requirements are as follows:

- The name and address of the distillery, supplier or bottler
- The country of origin
- The quantity of product in the bottle (for example, 33cl or 750ml). It is advisable to use the '℮' symbol to show that the average value of quantity meets that which is advertised
- The ABV of the product
- Allergy declarations. Take care with these. Distillation can remove most of the allergenic compounds from botanicals, but not all. Cold compounding does not. Do your research!

Note that for gin, there is no need to state a 'use by' date as this regulation only applies to alcohol of 10 per cent ABV or lower.

The Portman Group

The Portman Group describes itself as 'the alcohol social responsibility body and regulator of alcohol marketing in the UK'. It effectively polices alcohol branding and marketing to ensure responsible best practice, and to protect those who are under age and vulnerable. It hears challenges and complaints, and publishes its findings. For example, your label cannot be of a style that might appeal to children, and your advertisements cannot make such claims that your product increases attractiveness or enhances sexual ability.

You are strongly advised to ensure that all your labelling, packaging, branding and advertising adheres to the Portman Group's codes of practice. Full details can be found at www.portmangroup.org.uk.

LICENSING IN OTHER COUNTRIES

America

In America there are three levels of red tape that craft distillers have to observe: federal, state and local. The starting point for all distillers is to obtain a federal licence or permit to manufacture and sell alcohol. The first port of call is the Alcohol and Tobacco Tax and Trade Bureau (TTB) at the US Department of the Treasury. Here applicants must first qualify with TTB by *applying for a permit to operate*. This can be done online. Beyond that it comes down to checking with the state in which the distilling is to take place, as each state has its own laws about craft distilling.

Canada

The federal requirements for applying for a distilling permit in Canada are quite similar to those in the United States. In Canada, the law requires people to obtain a licence to distil spirits called the Excise Act 2001. This can be found via the Canada Revenue Agency at the Canada Government. Aside from federal regulations, distillers will also need to consider provincial or territorial alcohol manufacturing regulations, and will need to apply for permits relating to the territory in which the business is based.

Australia

Alcohol licensing legislation in Australia is developed independently in each state and territory, and administered through the relevant licensing authorities throughout the country. However, the starting point for the manufacture or storage of excisable alcohol products is to hold the appropriate excise licence. To use a still of any capacity to distil gin, an excise manufacturer licence must be held. It can be obtained from the Australian Tax Office at the Australian Government. Alcohol manufacturers should also check state liquor licensing laws, and with health agencies.

CONCLUSION

As you can see, there is a lot to consider under licensing and regulation. When applying for licences, do ensure that you allow enough time for everything to come through. We would recommend at least a two-month period to ensure that you have everything in place before you start making and selling any gin.

Moreover, it is advisable to design compliance into all your processes and procedures right from the start, as it can be difficult and expensive to correct them afterwards.

Finally, we stress again that nothing in this chapter should be considered legally binding, or as formal legal advice, nor does it claim to be complete in all respects regarding complying with the law in your country, including the UK. You remain responsible for all your own licensing, and for ensuring that you meet appropriate national and local standards and regulations.

CHAPTER 10

THE FUTURE OF GIN

THE GIN RENAISSANCE

The twenty-first-century 'Ginaissance', as it has become known, has certainly shaken off the dusty image gin once had, and has been reborn. No more is it the preserve of Noel Coward, Winston Churchill or your grandmother reaching for her favourite tipple of Gordon's and tonic, which she first enjoyed in 1941. Gin has been refreshed and revitalized. It has stumbled into the sunshine of the new millennium blinking and ready for a resurgence. Gin bars are the hangouts of young people, mostly twenty-something, and this trend of young people drinking gin is set to continue. They've come for the Instagrammable drink, the snapshot that conveys how fashionable they are. Others arrive to peruse the extensive gin menu, often containing more than 100 gins, and sample a few with forensic ferocity. Finally the dedicated fans come to discuss the botanicals that make up the recipe with which they are presented by the ever more flamboyant and knowledgeable bar staff. Or should we call them mixologists now?

Gin is undergoing a renaissance and has reinvented itself as the fashionable new drink of the young and the slightly older! Gin cocktails are making gin more accessible than ever.

THE MAGIC GIN TOUCH

The increase in gin sales has led to a revival of the British pub, which has been in decline for a number of years. Gin sales in 2019 registered a 40 per cent increase in pubs according to the Wine and Spirit Trade Association (WSTA). In the same year the UK saw 320 more pubs open than in 2018, according to the Office of National Statistics. The rise in pubs marked a dramatic turnaround compared to the previous nine years when pubs in the UK declined by an average of 732 each year. Some of this revival has been put down to the incredibly well stocked gin bars many pubs now offer, which are attracting young people to come and experiment or enjoy a cocktail in a way they can't do at home.

Increased gin sales have led to a revival of the British pub, which has been in decline for a number of years according to the Wine and Spirit Trade Association.

Drinks companies and landlords are having to ensure that they keep on trend and up to date with the fast-changing preferences of their customers. In the future these customers will increasingly look to engage with brands that offer them authenticity, a quality brand experience, and which deliver against values that they hold important. To begin, let's focus on how the gin renaissance has created some surprising outcomes for drinkers, the drinks sector, and the British economy as a whole.

Gin's Premium Status

The evolution of the gin drinker reflects a trend for spending more on meaningful experiences. This is driving the premium status of gin. Consumers appear keen to treat themselves to an experience when they choose a gin and tonic or a gin cocktail. They are hoping for a fabulous-looking drink in a pub or bar environment, mixed with a premium tonic and decorated with sweets, herbs, fruits or flowers. Alternatively they are looking for a re-creation of it at

The premiumization of gin has led to the increase in sales of high-end gins to drinkers wishing for a luxury indulgence.

home, where perhaps they've indulged in an upmarket gin and wish to fashion themselves as the hippest profession of all, a mixologist.

The premiumization of gin is presenting a huge opportunity for gin distillers. There is no denying that it has been responsible for propelling gin to unprecedented heights in mature markets such as the UK. According to the International Wine and Spirits Record (IWSR), one of the leading sources of data and analysis on the beverage alcohol market, data concerning global gin consumption, looked at in different price bands, is particularly revealing. The Compound Annual Growth Rate (CAGR) for gin sales in the ultra-premium segment between 2013 and 2018 was an incredible 50.1 per cent. This is considered a dramatic and unique growth by the industry.

What is more revealing is that the ISWR forecast growth for the period between 2018 and 2023 for upmarket gin brands is similarly positive. Focusing on that data reveals that the CAGR for premium, super-premium and ultra-premium gin is 10.4 per cent, 13.9 per cent and 17.6 per cent respectively, according to the IWSR. This may come as a surprise to some, who have seen the mass appeal of the lower end of the market as exemplified by the desire by many to drink any gin as long as it's pink, aided along the way by the explosion of The Pinkster gin and the huge popularity of Gordon's pink gin.

PROVENANCE AND AUTHENTICITY

It is very clear that consumers' demand for unique and craft-focused drinks is growing. It is visible every day as another flavoured gin is released or another artisan distillery opens to much coverage in the traditional media or effusive posts on social media. Demand has transformed the industry, and will continue to do so. Small distillers have been crucial to the gin market's growth – the emergence of the craft gin movement, emphasizing its provenance credentials, was a perfectly timed zeitgeist to coincide with the global rise of social media and consumers' growing interest in authentic brand stories.

Provenance

Consumers are becoming more discerning and they want to know the provenance behind their drinks and where they are made. A strong interest in the provenance of what we consume emerged from

PROVENANCE IN IDENTICAL GINS

The well-regarded Drinks by the Dram, which delivers 30ml tasting samples through the post, has found great success with one of its selection boxes. The specially curated tasting set offers five different gins, all made to precisely the same recipe. However, one element that does change is the provenance of the junipers. One iteration of the gin uses junipers from Italy, another junipers from Bulgaria, a third from Macedonia, and from Serbia and from Croatia. It highlights that few drinkers take too much note of the provenance of the juniper berries in a gin, as they are often too dazzled by the tree moss, barbecued rosemary or whatever new botanical is being added to the list of ingredients. When sampling the five varieties a drinker is made very aware of how incredibly different the gin can taste. Some junipers give the gin a more citrusy flavour, others a more earthy or floral flavour. What it clearly shows is that it all comes down to the 'terroir' of the region where the junipers were grown.

Provenance in gin has become much desired. One drinks provider offers a tasting pack of identical gins, but each is made with junipers sourced from different countries for drinkers to appreciate the difference in 'terroir'.

another sector, long before it reached the gin category. In Britain we have long been interested in knowing from where our food originates and how it reached our plate. This in turn became a powerful marketing tool with which to differentiate and promote brands.

The desire for provenance has now moved on to gin. As more and more small batch gins reach the market, interest in the botanicals and other ingredients used in them has risen. Many more gin drinkers are better informed and understand the complexities involved in the making of gin. This leads them to want transparency, and an understanding of what is going into their drink. They wish to glean the knowledge and also the provenance.

Consumers are much more aware of the botanicals involved in gin making, partly because distillers are much more open about what they are using. It has become a point of differentiation and conversation. Sky Wave Gin has found that when it has taken its gin to markets, festivals and tastings, the passion with which the team has been met by consumers is astounding. Gin enthusiasts desire the knowledge and detail of what makes one gin they are drinking taste different from another. In turn, this has provided a timely marketing tool. Distilleries, working to create a loyal following, are using the provenance of their botanicals to draw in drinkers. Some specify botanicals coming from a certain region, or sourced in a specific way. Sky Wave Gin uses blackberries foraged from the Oxfordshire hedgerows near to the distillery, as one of its thirteen botanicals. It also makes a point of using locally grown rhubarb in its raspberry and rhubarb gin. Rhubarb growers are paid with bottles of gin, which works very happily for both sides. The same arrangement goes for the local Oxfordshire apple growers who provide the fruit for Sky Wave's spiced apple gin liqueur. The team behind Edinburgh Gin makes a point of ensuring they can source many of their botanicals from Scotland. Twisting Spirits, based in Gloucestershire, highlights that they forage for Douglas fir needles, used in one of their gins, which they gather from a secret selection of trees.

The provenance of Oxfordshire is very important to Sky Wave Gin. Blackberries from local hedgerows are foraged in season and used as one of the thirteen botanicals in our London Dry.

Oxfordshire apple growers provide the fruit for our spiced apple gin liqueur, enhancing our sense of place and authenticity. Whole fresh fruit is used, rather than dried fruit or flavourings sourced from beyond the county.

Authenticity

The discerning craft gin drinker not only wants to know the provenance of their favourite artisan gin, but also wants to understand the authenticity of the product. There has sprung up a certain 'train spotter' geekiness to some passionate gin drinkers, which is only to be lauded and embraced! They carry around with them the most astonishing range of facts about their favourite (or least favourite) gins, and often wish to discuss them with distillers, while learning all the details about that new business with which they are engaging.

Gin companies have realized that one of the most powerful marketing tools they have is the origin and creation of their gin recipes and the production methods they use. When it comes to the story behind a gin, every craft gin drinker wants to hear it. In their eyes, the big brand names, churning out millions of litres of gin a year from a stainless-steel factory, have little appeal. They can't relate to the soul, the passion, the authenticity of their favourite gin. Rather they want to hear about the journey on which the craft distillers have travelled. They want to know the adversities faced, the triumphs won, the quirkiness around the founding of the distillery, and overall, they want to hear about the human passion and endeavour that imbue the gin they are drinking. In turn they want to tell those stories to others, to share their passion and their knowledge.

Sky Wave Gin began as a surprise fiftieth birthday present. A trip to gin school led to the discovery of a fabulous recipe. A passing dabble became a serious job, and eighteen months after launching, the two partners won The World's Best Contemporary Gin 2020. It was unprecedented. And everyone wants to know what the name means. There's a story behind that, too – it can be found on the back label of the bottle! The botanicals used in Sky Wave gin were chosen very carefully and with specific reasons. The distillers wanted them to reflect the Oxfordshire countryside in which the gin is distilled, but also the more far-flung countries where the two owners have had many adventures, from mountain climbing to driving across the Sahara, wing walking to scuba diving. The foraged blackberries represent a deep bond with the landscape around the distillery from where they are gathered. The very act of picking blackberries is imbued with a sense of place and, often, childhood memories of stained and sticky fingers, scratched legs and sunny days. To stay connected with the county in which Sky Wave Gin is created, the distillate is cut with Blenheim Palace Natural Mineral Water. The historic birthplace of Winston Churchill is just a few kilometres from the distillery. Sky Wave is proud to have built strong relationships with local fruit growers, who enjoy trading their rhubarb and apples for bottles of finished gin featuring their fruit.

Other artisan gins all have their own story, be it the ancient recipe dug out of a great grandmother's cookery book, or a despondent potato farmer who felt disenfranchized by selling his vegetables through faceless supermarkets, and turned to using his potatoes to create alcohol instead, developing it over time into gin.

Authenticity is much sought after in the gin world. The story of a how a gin went from zero to the World's Best Contemporary Gin in eighteen months is much enjoyed by Sky Wave Gin drinkers.

Gin companies have realized that one of the most powerful marketing tools they have is the origin and creation of their gin recipes and the production methods they use.

The fruit grown and delivered by local apple growers is repaid with gin, rather than money, reviving the age-old bartering system and maintaining a sense of provenance.

SEVENTEENTH-CENTURY AUTHENTICITY

Pinnock Gin from Warwickshire wanted to demonstrate a strong local provenance. The eleven botanicals include quince from Warwickshire, Cotswold lavender, and honey from Kineton, the village that is home to Pinnock. Kineton is situated close to Edge Hill where the famous Civil War battle took place in 1642. Owner and distiller Daniel Beckett wanted to draw on the history of the area for his gin, and managed to find an old recipe from the same era, for a drink similar to gin. The 450-year-old recipe provided the inspiration for some of the botanicals, as well as the font for the label. The name 'Pinnock' comes from the cottage where Daniel lives, and means 'house sparrow', which is also represented on the label.

Using ancient recipes can help with a sense of authenticity. This gin draws on a recipe derived from the seventeenth century, and was an inspiration for some of the botanicals.

Geography is another great source of provenance and authenticity, drawing in the enthusiast gin drinker to support their local gin. From Penzance Gin to Harrogate Gin, many are named after the town or county from which they originate. The branding and design will often reflect those geographic roots, too. The branding for Penzance Gin is created in the Art Deco style and portrays Penzance Jubilee Pool, an iconic art deco sea-water lido in the town. The distillers took inspiration for their modern-day gin from the Art Deco era, which influenced the architecture of the lido and the type of gin to which they aspire.

The geographical positioning of an artisan gin can draw on many sectors of the gin-drinking population. There are those who were born in the county or town of the gin, there are those who have holidayed in the place and want to take a small part of it home with them, and there are those who choose the gin for its aspirational overtones. They want to live there, or to holiday there, or to be seen as part of the set of people who just 'know' it.

Geography is another great source of provenance and authenticity, drawing in the enthusiast gin drinker to support their local gin.

These distillers took inspiration for their modern-day gin from the Art Deco era, which influenced the architecture of the lido in Penzance that features on their label.

The business of craft gin is also hugely attractive to a whole swathe of deeply enthusiastic gin drinkers because the distillers love to talk about *how* they make their gin, and the gin drinkers love to *hear* about it. To start with, the passion that distillers show their stills is infectious. They are carefully crafted, sometimes shipped from distant countries, often individually designed, and always lovingly named. Sky Wave Gin has two stills: a large production still named Tessie, after our first and faithful spaniel, and a developmental still named Tilly, which arrived around the same time as our playful new spaniel puppy.

The boom in the sale of craft gin is partly because the drinkers experience the distilling process vicariously. They have met the distillers at gin festivals, they've read about the process on gin websites, and they've seen the pictures of the polished, traditional copper-pot still or fabulous stainless-steel creation from which the gin they have in their kitchen has originated. At Sky Wave Gin, the process of distilling is often filmed in tiny snippets and posted on social media, and hugely enjoyed by all the followers. Large gin industries can't offer that very personal, close up involvement, the handmade element of the creation of the gin right down to the moment it is cut by taste, not machines, nor the handwriting of the bottle labels. It is this proximity to production and the very vital human involvement that inspires drinkers to choose a craft gin, and which keeps this sector of the gin market growing into the future.

Gin enthusiasts feel an affinity with their favourite craft gins as they often meet and talk to the distillers themselves at one of the many markets or gin festivals held across Britain.

CRAFT DISTILLERIES INCREASE

The number of distilleries in the UK has surged as craft gin continues to grow in popularity. Despite the naysayers, in 2020 gin is still surging ahead in popularity according to pub landlords and industry figures. This has given confidence to more and more small, craft distilleries to set up and try and elbow their way into the increasingly popular gin scene. But they all seem to manage to do it, however crowded it seemingly becomes.

In 2019, the number of distilleries jumped by 20 per cent to 246, up from 205 the previous year according to accountancy firm UHY Hacker Young. The number of distilleries has grown every year since 2011. In 2019 more new distilleries opened in England than in Scotland. This marked the first time that the number of English distilleries overtook those in Scotland, on the back of the booming gin trade – although Scotland still contains the higher proportion of larger distilleries as those in England tend to be small.

Consumers are willing to pay premium prices for craft gin, and the number of new distillery entrants to the market can be seen to reflect two trends. There are the passionate distillers and gin lovers who want to craft the best gin they can for their discerning audience. They've been able to enter the wonderous world of flavour, chemistry and creation due to the licensing laws changing in 2009. It meant that distilleries producing any amount of gin, from small to large, were able to be licensed.

The other type of distiller that has entered the market since the licensing laws changed, are the entrepreneurs. They have their eye on the prize. They have been attracted to the spirits sector as they have recognized that big drinks firms are eyeing smaller 'authentic brands'. Mergers and acquisitions activity in this sector have been strong. It is thought that growth won't continue forever, but currently domestic and overseas consumers' demand for UK craft spirits hasn't been met. Industry experts believe that the trend for authentic local artisan gin is here to stay, and that will continue to draw entrepreneurs and investors into the craft spirits industry.

In the eleven years since the opening up of the distilling market, the spirits sector has diversified beyond a handful of large distillers to a market now represented by producers of all shapes and sizes in both the USA and the UK. Yet consolidation is becoming a growing trend. For a look into the future we need only turn our sights to Sipsmith. The partnership behind this brand pioneered the craft gin rise by challenging the long-held position of HMRC that it would only license distilleries operating a still with a capacity of no less than 1,800ltr. Sipsmith rewrote the rule book by winning their battle in 2009 to use smaller stills in their quest to distil the best London Dry Gin, and hence the craft gin market was born. However, in 2016 the London-based company was purchased by Beam Suntory, a global drinks company that also owns Roku, which describes itself as a Japanese craft gin. It must be hoped that the marketing and demand for these corporate-owned 'craft' brands will remain the same.

INVESTING IN CRAFT GIN

Pernod Ricard, the Paris-based drinks company, announced in March 2020 that it was making a significant investment in the ultra-premium KI NO BI Kyoto Dry Gin. The investment will be used to build a new state of the art distillery to meet demand. KI NO BI is a small-batch, artisanal gin reflecting its Japanese culture. It is distilled at Japan's first dedicated gin distillery in Kyoto. Pernod Ricard, which has already partnered with ultra-premium gin Monkey 47 from Germany, recognized the entrepreneurs behind KU NO BI, and said it wanted to optimise the growth opportunity in ultra-premium gin.

EXPORTS

The rest of the world is helping to fuel the 'ginaissance'. The taste for gin has gone global, and this is part of the future for our spirit. The Germans are particularly fond of their craft gins, and have a passion for British ones, too. Just a short time spent on social media will reveal the huge followings that Germans, Scandinavians and the Spanish have for gin, with the Italians and Americans not far behind. The UK gin industry saw export sales increase by 9 per cent to £672 million pounds in 2019, according to HMRC figures, while home sales of gin in the UK totalled £2.6 billion in the year to June 2019, according to the latest statistics from the Wine and Spirits Trade Association (WSTA), with more than 82 million bottles sold. More gin is exported around the world than beef, wheat or beer, according to the WSTA, with gin sales abroad worth 14 per cent more than British beer. British beer sales abroad totalled £590m in 2019. It is interesting to note that almost half of Britain's gin exports go to the EU.

Home-grown gin producers are gearing up to take on new export markets in the future. One of the most exciting new markets is China. As the country continues to develop its taste for premium Western goods, gin is perfectly placed to do well on the continent. Sky Wave is one of many gin companies investigating export opportunities to the East.

INNOVATION

The gin market is fast moving and always changing. New gins spring up virtually every week, promoting new regions and espousing new botanicals. The customers that are being targeted are seemingly often changing. Where vodka was once the innovator, with an extensive array of flavours and dedicated vodka bars offering everything from chilli vodka to Mars Bar vodka, the speed and creativity witnessed in the gin sector is breath taking. Pink gin is no longer a niche offshoot, it is a rapidly expanding segment in its own right. Major brands that were slightly behind the craft gin curve, played catch-up to release their own version of a pink gin, including Gordon's, Beefeater, Bloom and Pinkster. UK retailer Marks & Spencer has partnered with The Old Curiosity to release its own range of colour-changing gins. Edible 22-carat gold flakes now pervade a number of gins, offering that all-important 'wow' factor and adding even more glamour to the gin-drinking experience.

Botanicals have been selected from far and wide in the search for an innovative new flavour. Black olives were chosen for Gin Eva, a Spanish gin that combined them with just two other botanicals to create a world award-winning gin. Ki No Bi Gin from the Kyoto Distillery blends the all-important provenance with

Innovation is helping to drive the growth of gin. Elephant Gin uses a range of unusual botanicals such as baobab fruit and buchu plant.

botanicals not commonly found in gin, including bamboo leaves and wood chips sourced from close to its Japanese distillery. Elephant Gin has been boosting conservation efforts for Africa's elephants since 2013. In its aged edition there is a range of unusual botanicals such as baobab fruit, buchu plant (similar to blackcurrant), African wormwood, lion's tail (a broadleaf evergreen large shrub) and devil's claw (a plant that bears distinctive, hooked fruit), which are combined with more traditional botanicals to produce its gin.

Craft gins, often made in small batches, have the agility to test and trial new flavourings, bringing out new limited editions – gins with a short production run that can experiment with new botanicals more nimbly than the big drinks companies.

Savoury Gins

Industry experts are predicting that savoury gins are set to be one of the new trends for 2020 and beyond. There's a huge increase in more vegetable/savoury flavours, particularly in gin. Some of this could be a small backlash to the huge popularity of sugary, sweet pink gins. Savoury cocktails, offering subtle herbaceous flavours, and even salt or spice, have risen from a niche oddity to a menu mainstay.

So what is a savoury gin? Well, the good news is that there are already a lot out there from which to choose. Essentially, it is a gin that offers gentle herbaceous undertones of salinity and crispness. At the 2020 World Gin Awards, Sky Wave Gin was named the World's Best Contemporary Gin, and the judges described it as having 'good salinity'. Sweet gins are not to everyone's taste, and the rise in savoury gins is being met with the development of beautifully savoury mixers – for example, Franklin & Sons' olive and rosemary tonic.

THREATS TO THE FUTURE OF GIN

The future of gin does face some threats. America is the largest importer of British gin, with sales reaching £675m in 2018. However, the IWSR's data suggests that US consumer demand for gin is waning, and the forecast for 2018–2023 is flat. It is worth noting that across the board, sales of spirits are increasing in the USA. Americans spent more than $51.1bn on them in 2018, but their spending habits are moving away from white varieties to dark, flavour-filled liquids such as whisky and tequila. This plays into the 'rum theory', bandied about by journalists looking for a new story and retailers looking for a new trend to push to customers, that rum is the 'next big thing'. But in reality this tipple is not as appealing as gin. It is less versatile, less pleasing visually, and in Britain at least has associations with hoary old sea-dog types of drinker, from its history as a sailors' drink. Having said that, gin distillers shouldn't take their eye off the ball.

IN CONCLUSION

In conclusion, the gin boom is most definitely not over yet. Peak gin is still to come. The recent William Grant & Sons Trending 2020 report forecast that gin would overtake vodka to become the biggest spirit category in the UK's pubs and bars in the same year, finding that the spirit was now (2020) worth £2bn to the nation's on and off trades. When it comes to overseas demand for UK craft spirits, that has not been met yet either, so exports will continue to rise. There is much opportunity and optimism for the craft gin distiller at home and abroad.

However, gin must be careful not to repeat the mistakes of its closest rival, vodka, which despite its premium brands has not seen such popularity as gin in recent years. Like vodka, gin is seeing ever-more obscure and radically flavoured expressions overcrowd the gin market. Consumers may suffer flavour fatigue, and innovation may dry up. Moreover, flavoured gins are still an entry point for new gin drinkers, who may get a taste for it and move on to more classic gins, which will broaden out the classic gin category. As can be seen from the growth patterns at the beginning of this chapter, the market will settle into good quality gins, premium and super premium, with a solid space reserved for savoury gins and flavoured gins and the role they play.

The gin boom is not over, as forecasters predict gin will become the biggest spirits category in UK pubs in 2020.

The vast array of gins currently on offer provides a range of entry points for new gin drinkers.

The future looks bright for craft gin drinkers enjoying authentic, artisan gin produced by small distillers, displaying incredible dedication to the craft.

The trend for authentic local artisan gin looks to be here to stay, bolstered by its growing fan base, and that will continue to tempt entrepreneurs and investors into the craft spirits industry. So there is a justifiable sense of optimism for small distillers, displaying incredible dedication to the craft and its creative, reborn future.

RECOMMENDED SUPPLIERS

We thought it would be helpful to have a list of suppliers that we have used or have been recommended to us, to get you off to a flying start with your gin project. Where possible we try our hardest to support local businesses.

EQUIPMENT

Stills

Iberian Coppers S.A., Portugal: copper-alembic.com/en/
Lovebrewing, UK online: lovebrewing.co.uk
Hillybilly Stills, Kentucky, USA: hillbillystills.com

Alcoholmeters and Thermometers

Lovebrewing, UK online: lovebrewing.co.uk
Many other online outlets.

Drums and Containers

Smiths of the Forest of Dean Ltd: smithsofthedean.co.uk
Amazon: amazon.co.uk

Beakers

Jaytec: jaytecglass.co.uk
Amazon: amazon.co.uk

Scales

Farnell: uk.farnell.com

DISTILLING

Neutral Spirit

Master of Malt: masterofmalt.com
Kimia (will need licences): kimiauk.co.uk

Botanicals

JustIngredients: justIngredients.co.uk
BuyWholeFoodsOnline: buywholefoodsonline.co.uk

Online Calculator and Resource

Distillique: distillique.co.za

CUTTING

Water

Your local spring water
Distilled water online

BOTTLING

Bottles

Kefla: kefla.de
Rawlings: rawlingsbristol.co.uk
World of Bottles: worldofbottles.co.uk
Drinkstuff: drinkstuff.com

Corks

Corks will usually be supplied by bottle suppliers. Standard corks will be synthetic.
For bespoke all-natural cork stoppers: Just Wood: justwood.com

Bottling Machines and Filters

Vigo Ltd: vigoltd.com

Seals

World of Bottles: worldofbottles.co.uk

Labels – Design and Printing

KMS Litho Ltd: kmslitho.co.uk
Daymark Labels: daymark.co.uk
LabelService: labelservice.co.uk

Duty Stamps

HMRC: gov.uk/guidance/alcohol-licensing

PACKAGING

Leaflets/ Printers

Use your local printers, e.g. Bicester Print: bicesterprint.com

SHIPPING

Packaging Suppliers, Branded Boxes and Bubblewrap

Kite Packaging: kitepackaging.co.uk

Quickbox: quickbox.co

Applegate (central marketplace for obtaining suppliers and quotes): applegate.co.uk

POSTAL AND SHIPPING

Royal Mail: parcel.royalmail.com

DPD: dpdlocal-online.co.uk

UPS: ups.com/gb/en/Home.page

INDEX